2016

For Rina
A woman of
depth and integrity,

Fondly,
Ruth

# CHOOSE COURAGE:

## Step Into the Life You Want

---

By Ruth M. Schimel, Ph.D.

# Copyright

CHOOSE COURAGE: Step into the Life You Want
Copyright © 2013 by Ruth M. Schimel, Ph.D.

Cover Design by Blen Getahun of BlenDesigns
([www.blendesigns.com](www.blendesigns.com))

ISBN-13: 978-1490343303

ISBN-10: 149034330X

# Limit of Liability and Disclaimer

The publisher and author have made their best efforts to prepare this book for your effective use and benefit. By all means use your good judgment and intuition to make the most of your experience with it.

They make no representation or warranties to the accuracy or completeness of the contents of this book. Any implied warranties, merchantability, and fitness for a particular purpose are also disclaimed.

This book is meant to be informational and educational. As such, it does not constitute psychological or medical advice. Bear in mind that the advice and strategies may not be suitable for your situation. You should therefore consult with a professional as appropriate.

Neither the author nor publisher shall be liable for any loss of profit or any other commercial damages, including, but not limited to special, incidental, or consequential other damages.

# About the Author

Though I may not seem a neatly-defined expert to some, my focus has consistently been helping people realize their true capacities. This commitment reflects my parent's values as well; my engineer father taught high school youth trades in the South Bronx and my mother chose at mid-life to teach in Harlem. Learning about and strengthening the ties that bring us all together for mutual benefit and progress continue to this day.

Since 1983, I have been serving over 1000 career and life management consulting clients of all ages, backgrounds, and education. Building beyond conventional approaches, I provide original materials, inspiration, and tailored guidance that promote clients' self-sufficiency and progress. www.ruthschimel.com

Also supporting my commitment to others' professional and personal development, I speak and write, train and facilitate groups. In 1998, I conceived and now manage The Schimel Lode to promote collaboration and innovation for the public good in the Washington, D.C. area. www.TheSchimelLode.net

Previously, I was a management consultant and taught a variety of human resource subjects at Georgetown, American, George Washington, and Marymount Universities. In a prior incarnation, I served as a diplomat in the Department of State, Ecuador, Guatemala, and India. I did a range of work from intelligence analysis to manage the consular section in Calcutta.

Honoring the complexity of human beings, my interests continue to be interdisciplinary. As you'll see expressed in *Choose Courage,* they include the arts, sciences, and social sciences. My degrees are:

- Ph.D. in public management, workforce development, and gerontology from George Washington University

- M.A. in behavioral science, government, and personnel, also from GWU.

- B.S. in industrial and labor relations from Cornell

Though the theme of courage for my doctoral dissertation actually came through a vision, it unites my passions, interests, education, skills, and experience, just as I encourage my clients to do. From the research, I know that dealing with a mob in Calcutta or confronting a thief on the street was not courageous — maybe foolhardy, in fact. But meaning what I say and doing what I mean, as Horton the Elephant said, comes much closer to my new, 21$^{st}$-century definition of courage.

# Dedication

In honor of Abraham Lincoln Schimel and Beatrice Schimel whose actions reflected their values:

Pop was an electrical engineer who taught high school students trades for self-sufficiency in the South Bronx. Mom was a volunteer community organizer who returned to school while working full-time; she completed her bachelor's degree with honors at 50 and then asked to teach in Harlem.

They planted me here, showing by example how to be original and responsible. They also supported my choices, whether or not they echoed their experience and expectations.

# Acknowledgements

The dictionary can be a source of subtle, significant direction as I've learned in renewing the meaning of courage. Look up acknowledgement and you'll find *confess, admit existence, reality or truth of, recognition of, express gratitude for and report receipt of.* All these aspects are woven into the recent riches I've received from:

Kathleen Sindell, Ph.D., superb editorial and technical guide as well as collaborator for publishing *Choose Courage: Step into the Life You Want.* A successful author, she brings joy, knowledge, skill, resourcefulness, and insight to this challenging, exciting process.

Ivan Sindell, PMP, her partner and my sometimes technical guru. He mitigates my various levels of computer ignorance with patience, generosity, and expertise.

Andrew Winter, close friend and colleague of decades. He is the main source of the superb, rich photographic metaphors for the book as well as some candid shots of me.

Zeke Mekonnen, dearest Bro and cheerleader. He also made his fine photographs available, now and generously for future publications.

Marcia Shannon, dearest Sis and cheerleader, who encouraged effective marketing.

Ani Bustamante, the ironic, clever source of most of the thought-provoking, original drawings and other art.

Amé Solomon, caring, capable cousin. She has shared valuable family discernment as well as her playful photographs of the children and nature.

Amelia Moser, another cousinly photographer whom I also cherish.

Blen Getahun, the graphic designer of the cover and photographer, who came through quickly, effectively, and creatively with a dynamic, inspiring cover and lively photographs of me.

Roz Paris, childhood friend and fellow "clip artist," and J.W. Wohlever, board member of The Schimel Lode, who commented helpfully on aspects of a much earlier version.

A raft of other friends, colleagues, and connections who discussed, challenged, explored, supported, and encouraged me. Among them were Carole E. Horn, Amy Swauger, Nancy Rawles, Kathy DeBoe, Kathy Ramsperger, Jeanne Svikhart, Richard Bodane, Linda Hill, Theo Broekhof, Peg Blechman, Sandy Vogelgesang, Lily Garcia, Shari Garmise, Greg Lipscomb, Adrienne Umansky, Susan Morris, and Anita DeVivo.

The vision for and aspects of *Choose Courage* emerged from the chrysalis of my doctoral dissertation which, I believe, was user friendly despite academic requirements. For that nontraditional, interdisciplinary outcome combining philosophy and psychology, I thank my Ph.D. committee at the then School of Government and Business Administration of The George Washington University. They were Bayard Catron, Steve Chitwood, and Cynthia McSwain.

# Table of Contents

xiv

xvii

# Preface

Most non-fiction books are linear, but life is not. To honor these realities, *Choose Courage* is designed to serve your varying interests and to reflect a purpose of my life to promote human strengths and possibilities.

The new, viable definition of courage that permeates the book is holistic. While this inspiring platform provides the foundation and focus, many aspects of the six Steps can stand alone. Yet the relationships among the parts are clear, wherever you start and return.

Just as meaning and opportunities emerge through interaction, *Choose Courage* provides connective tissue for developing your strengths and taking effective, incremental action. In contrast to many how-to and self-help books, other people's stories are kept to a minimum. Rather, you'll see how you and your stories are the stars, proving your capacity for courage.

The self-determined process for using this book is as original as its 21st-century definition of courage, based on actual doctoral research with everyday people. Instead of the heroic clichés and vague ideas into which the word courage often devolves, this definition is designed to be used in daily life.

As with the fluid design of the book, the definition of courage is based on a process of becoming. Not a characteristic available only to a brave few nor an isolated act that must be repeated for credibility, this definition is accessible to almost everyone as life is lived.

Becoming courageous involves the willingness to realize your true capacities by going *through* discomfort, fear, anxiety, or suffering and taking wholehearted, responsible action. Since the words we use tend to define us and our actions, each one is clarified in the book to support your understanding and progress.

For added depth, attention to allied aspects is also paid. They include authenticity, commitment, passion, and vocation.

From my own life, I know it's easier to provide inspiring language and guidance than to apply them. Honoring this reality is another focus of *Choose Courage: Step Into the Life You Want*: taking realistic small steps, supported with an array of tools that can be tailored to specific situations.

Verve and entertainment from the arts enrich *Choose Courage* as well. Photographs, poetry, quotes, drawings, humor, links to eclectic, lively sources, and other ways to engage you for personal and professional development are included.

For a taste of how the book unfolds and where to dip in as needs and interests arise, here is a summary of the Six Steps:

**Step One Imagining and Preparing for Your Journey:** prepares you for action, answering why you should bother to access your capacity for courage. It shows how an array of often messy, uncontrollable influences makes life naturally complex. In spite of them, attention is given to where you might make a difference and how you may choose to act.

**Step Two Getting Ready to Express your Courage:** helps you get ready to realize your courage through being authentic, entrusting yourself to someone or something beyond you through commitment, appreciating the emotions that energize your passions, and expressing yourself through what you value, or vocation.

**Step Three Identifying Internal Barriers to Progress:** shows how to identify and start to wrestle with internal barriers to progress, including discomfort, fear, anxiety, guilt, suffering and imprints from the past.

**Step Four Surpassing Internal Barriers:** provides concrete ways to transcend internal barriers, releasing hope and energy for productive action and progress.

**Step Five Expressing Your Own Courage:** explains the new definition of courage based on original research, how it emerges, and a range of choices to make it work for you. You'll see how to access and appreciate your courage through your own stories.

**Step Six Taking Action:** supports your continuing voyage of choosing courage through strengthening cycles and additional opportunities for action. It includes reminders of the range of your own powers that contribute to meaning, engagement, and effective results.

Throughout, my commitment is to attend to life's realities, complexities, and paradoxes without being sidetracked from what's useful to you. I also want to provide encouragement and inspiration based on what is available in everyday life. To steal from an idea in process philosophy, how something is done determines what it becomes. And so, I hope I show how you can use *Choose Courage* as a continuing catalyst for realizing your true capacities and the life you want through small steps.

# STEP ONE:
# Imagining and Preparing for Your Own Journey

## What to Expect

The frequent use of the word courage could descend into a heroic cliché captured in stories of other people, exhortations, and vague definitions from various celebrities. Yet more than 186 million current entries on Google show the word still attracts great attention. No doubt that's because it holds the promise of human possibility. For you, such numbers may suggest that too much has already been said about the subject, even if you could easily capture the essence of it all.

As conversations and writing about courage continue, though, they can help you attend to valuable unfinished business. *Choose Courage: Step Into the Life You Want* offers this opportunity in new, specific ways, while honoring your already proven strengths and efforts — whether or not you appreciate them fully.

From the Greeks onward, there seems to be no proven definition to help individuals discover and strengthen their own courage. Hunger for such a map to the power within persists — otherwise, you'd probably not be reading this.

*Choose Courage* is the first book to provide:

- a new, practical definition based on actual research that makes courage available to almost anyone

- ways for you to hear and confirm your courage through your *own* stories

- varied material you can dip into at any point that meets your needs and interests — life is not as linear as a book

- serious and lighthearted presentation, including digestible summaries, illustrations, photography, poetry, and attention to daily realities

© *Photograph by Andrew Winter*

**Her high stretch reflects mental concentration, strength, and preparation.**

Navigating these especially anxious times is easier done with hope and inspiration. This book also provides tailored assistance to promote your persistence.

Starting with your capacity for courage marks an efficient path to your powers and potential. As Winston Churchill said, "*Courage is rightly esteemed the first of human qualities...because it is the quality which guarantees all others.*"

The original definition of courage you'll see a few pages later is based on the lives of everyday people. Instead of being a characteristic of just some special individuals or an isolated, dramatic act, the capacity for courage is within almost everyone. The process of becoming courageous is accessible to you regardless of education, gender, age, situation, or experience.

This book will suit you when you:

- are in transition

- seek greater meaning and feel curious about new possibilities in life and work

- believe your present situation and actions can be improved

- are tired of succumbing to fear, anxiety, and other limiting emotions

- progress best using ideas and tools appropriate to your own values and interests

- want to make intentional choices to improve your quality of life rather than just wait for chance or luck

However you relate to these opportunities, you may still wonder why another how-to book will make a positive difference when you've possibly already:

- read self-help and professional development books and articles, as well as taken workshops and courses

- completed your own self-improvement projects

- profited from participation in professional organizations and community groups

- consulted coaches, therapists, colleagues, family, or friends

Or maybe you've done none of this. No matter. To proceed, select what supports and engages you in *Choose Courage: Step Into the Life You Want.* Here you can expect to find guidance and inspiration to address what needs tending in your life. In the process, you'll learn *how to* access and express your courage, in your own ways.

To begin, let's be realistic. You'll probably never finish becoming your stronger self. When willing, you'll be empowering yourself and creating a better life over time. And even if there were a silver bullet, would you really want just one shot? Instead, you'll benefit from a range of opportunities and choices suited for changing needs, situations, and interests.

Use *Choose Courage* to realize more fully who you are and what you can do. You'll:

- build on whatever you've accomplished so far, starting from within where your real choices are

- go both wide and deep to catch what you want and need

- move beyond mulling to inspiring, manageable action

Let your capacity for courage and this book lead you forward using the following three processes.

# How to act from the inside out

Rather than depend on other people's experiences for guidance and inspiration, you'll see how your courageous actions and abilities are apparent in your own stories. They already show your capacities, waiting to be tapped — again and again — as you take manageable steps. Given the natural twists, turns, and static aspects of life, though, don't expect rapid or linear progress.

But when you persist, have patience, and use your sense of humor, you'll release the flow of progress. You'll see results from identifying and building on your proven strengths. Your confidence will increase, creating a source for continuing action. Paradoxically, as you become stronger, you'll be more likely to receive the support you want and need because others are attracted to your apparent potential and powers.

# How to access your courage: what you'll find within

The new definition is a gift that keeps on giving because you can invoke your courage whenever you choose. As a process of becoming, courage involves:

- *the willingness to realize your true capacities*

- *by going **through** discomfort, fear, anxiety, or suffering*

- *and taking wholehearted, responsible action.*

Intellectual, ethical, emotional, and spiritual aspects of this definition honor your whole self. Courage moves from what some consider a manly virtue to a universal one.

*Choose Courage* also explores the underlying meaning of courage based on heart. Connections with emotional vulnerability, openness, and inner strength reflect some of its rich paradoxes and complexities — as well as what really goes on in daily life.

(You'll find further discussion of the original research and ideas that support this definition throughout the book.)

## How to make the flexible format meet your needs

Books are linear, lives are not. *Choose Courage* is therefore designed so you can select any sequence that works for you. Though the new definition of courage provides a clear road map, the book offers multiple routes to suit various situations and styles. Your time is respected; useful guidance is available at any point without reading the whole book. As Little Jack Horner did in the nursery rhyme, just stick in your thumb (or any finger) at any point and pull out a plum.

Little Jack Horner, Illustration by William Wallace (1902).
*Image is in the public domain believed to be free to use without restriction in the US.*

An array of tools provides different alternatives for finding what works for you. Many can stand alone, available for separate use or in combination according to your needs. The voyage includes short "rest stops" for comfort, consideration, and exercise. Food metaphors and illustrations add humor, variety, and other psychic and sensual nutrition.

© *Photograph by Zeke Mekonnen*

***Even gentle gorillas take regular time out to think and restore themselves; studies show apes can set goals and follow through on them.***

So read and use *Choose Courage* in the sequence presented if that works for you. Or find in the table of contents and index whatever Step, subject, or section meets your specific needs and interests at a particular time. You can also just flip or scan the pages to see what catches your fancy. Using any approach that appeals, choose the speed and depth that works well for you.

As you create and enjoy your own rhythm of attention and action, the benefits will bring optimism and energy for continuing efforts. Since issues and opportunities often span professional and personal situations, your progress in one sphere can enrich the other. Just tune in fairly regularly to sustain momentum. As you no doubt have experienced, the more consistent your efforts, the more likely you'll see results.

## Possibilities for you

Throughout, *Choose Courage* shows you many ways forward, not one best way. Such variety attends to your unique qualities, needs, situations, and interests.

### *Find or create variety even when forms may seem similar.*

How to proceed may not always be obvious until you find something that encourages your action. Neither will quick fixes be likely or even appropriate. But each step you take will at least hold an opportunity for learning, practice, and progress. Over time, your self-respect strengthens. Delight and fun are part of this process that brings additional joy to your life.

*Choose Courage* is designed to take you beyond mulling, reading, and discussing. It recognizes that at some point just getting ready to move forward, without some follow through, can be self-deluding.

Benefit from the book's focus on *action* related to your needs, goals, and interests. Use the ideas, examples, and tools whole; alternatively, adapt or save them for another time. Do ignore aspects that don't speak to you. You won't find an imperious insistence on "just do it," which you obviously would have done already if you wanted to or could.

If something is not working for you, move on. Let each choice tell you something about what's important. That could help smooth your way through sometimes challenging situations. By all means, celebrate any progress in ways you'll enjoy.

Here is an outline of the six Steps of *Choose Courage* to use in whatever order works for you:

**Step One Imagining and Preparing for Your Journey:** prepares you for action, answering why you should bother to access your capacity for courage. It shows how an array of often messy, uncontrollable influences makes life naturally complex. In spite of them, attention is given to where you might make a difference and how you may choose to act.

*© Photograph by Zeke Mekonnen*

### *Though only a one-foot tall lookout for the clan, like this meerkat maybe you can at least look out for yourself and others.*

**Step Two Getting Ready to Express Your Courage:** helps you get ready to realize your courage through being authentic, entrusting yourself to someone or something beyond you through commitment, appreciating the emotions that energize your passions, and expressing yourself through what you value, or vocation.

**Step Three Identifying Internal Barriers to Progress:** shows how to identify and start to wrestle with internal barriers to progress, including discomfort, fear, anxiety, guilt, suffering, and imprints from the past.

**Step Four Surpassing Internal Barriers:** provides concrete ways to transcend internal barriers, releasing hope and energy for productive action and progress.

**Step Five Expressing Your Own Courage:** explains the new definition of courage based on original research, how it emerges, and a range of choices to make it work for you. You'll see how to access and appreciate your courage through your own stories.

© *Photograph by Zeke Mekonnen*

### *Bridges go both ways. Just choose a direction that works for you.*

*Note:* If interested in an extended metaphor of what courageous action entails see David McCullough's 2012 update of "The Great Bridge, the Epic Story of the Building of the Brooklyn Bridge" for an entrancing study of technology, human effort, and art.

**Step Six Taking Action:** supports your continuing voyage of choosing courage through strengthening cycles and additional opportunities for action. It includes reminders of the range of your own powers that contribute to meaning, engagement, and effective results.

# Why Bother?

*It takes courage to grow up and become who you really are.*
Poet, e.e. cummings

Bother because "nobody does it better," to adopt Carly Simon's well-known lyric. You know yourself best. And who has the strongest interest in your welfare?

You are also more likely to stay motivated to create the life you want. Certainly, family, teachers, colleagues, friends, partners, professional service providers, and mentors may contribute. Yet without your own insight and action, their assistance and commitment goes only so far.

"A limit of time is fixed for thee," according to Roman emperor-philosopher Marcus Aurelius. Unless reincarnation exists, making the most of your precious time on earth is in your hands. Intuitively you know how to use it well — and can get even better at it with practice. Making authentic choices will increase your powers and possibilities.

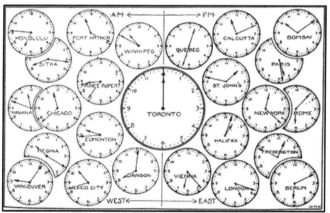

© *University of South Florida*

Finally, bodies and minds are designed for development. Otherwise, there can be a tendency toward stasis, immobility, and loss of possibilities, whatever one's age.

The inside argument for why bother honors the value of your energy and motivation for choice and action. The outside argument is change happens anyway, whether wanted or not. Without it, in fact, life would be quite predictable and likely boring.

"I could deal with boring," you say. Test that by remembering what has happened when you stayed stuck in your comfort zone. Did you eventually yearn for something, without knowing exactly what? The German sehnsucht for that captures in one word a feeling of intense yearning for something missing. That sense could disrupt seeming ease or even a successful life.

***However pleasant and relaxing, how long would you want to remain in such a scene without it losing attraction? How long before you want to move, to act?***

Whether or not you've felt such a yearning, your actual and symbolic muscles could weaken from disuse. How might you and others see you and your capabilities under such circumstances?

# Success

*Choose Courage* addresses both the inside and outside arguments for "why bother." This foundation helps you see how to influence situations, to shift them in your favor. It will help you know when to let go, plan, or adjust expectations. One way to prepare is to think about what a good outcome in a particular situation means to you. Some might call that success.

Just take about five minutes to jot down your own one or two definitions for success or what a good outcome in a particular situation would mean to you now. Your choices can be used for many purposes as well as to affirm or clarify a direction you choose now or later.

To encourage your exploration, here are tangible and intangible examples of what success might include:

- learning how to do something that brings you pleasure, meaning, or valuable results

- inspiring others to realize their strengths

- earning the money to support and sustain the life you want

- making a difference in or influencing your world

- creating a product, service, or art form that attracts, engages, or inspires others

- leading a family, group, community, or organization for everyone's benefit

Or see what you want to take away or adapt from American essayist and poet Ralph Waldo Emerson's definition of success:

> *To laugh often and much; to win the respect of intelligent people and affection of children; to earn the appreciation of honest critics and endure the*

*betrayal of false friends; to appreciate beauty; to find the best in others; to leave the world a bit better, whether by a healthy child, a garden patch or a redeemed social condition; to know even one life has breathed easier because I have lived. This is to have succeeded.*

Notice neither the bulleted list above nor Ralph Waldo Emerson's definition mentions money in itself. That's because research shows money alone may not sustain happiness, another measure of success to some. In fact, little of importance tends to stay the same over time, whether money, happiness, health, relationships, work, or success. Any can shift, ebbing and flowing, temporarily satisfying appetites that eventually yearn for that often insatiable four-letter word — more. Or different or better.

About money: Though disdainful of his view at the time, I remember my father saying it can mess up life. Too little, and frustrations and fears abound. Too much, however you define that, requires spending a lot of time figuring out what to do with it: protecting it and getting more of it. These concerns do not even address dealing with related anxieties as well as people who want a piece of your resources or your rich self.

Surfeit of money and other important things can lead to boredom for lack of challenge or obsessive accumulation of new things. That could result in endless cycles of repetition. A feeling of "is this all there is?" reminds of the emptiness of constantly filling up. Such results show why starting from the inside, or knowing who you are and can be as well as what you truly want, can be a firmer foundation for a good life. Money and other material markers of success alone may just not be enough to build and sustain a life of meaning, security, and pleasure.

# Failure

Considering how you define success may also bring failure to mind. But avoiding action or over thinking possible and actual failures can waste precious time. Both choices will likely postpone progress.

Should you find yourself focusing on past or expected failure, use any of the following questions to create strategies to avoid it and take effective action now:

- What one important lesson can you learn from previous detours and regrets?

- What specifically do you want to accomplish now?

- What main action can you take to promote a concrete, worthwhile outcome?

- What important information must you know or learn about to help decide when to continue with or quit a situation?

- How much time and resources are reasonable to devote?

- Who will help you progress?

Choose one or two of these questions that could elicit better ways to proceed or others that occur. Jot down some answers and ideas that immediately come to mind. From your brief notes, identify a few options, perhaps exploring them with someone you trust and respect. To activate your investment of thought and time in avoiding failure or something similar, take your first modest step within the next one or two days.

## Growth Mind Set

I hope you use the discussion of success and failure above to avoid a fixed mind set. That's what Carol Dweck says is thinking you have to be born with all the smarts and talents. Based on over three decades of research, the Stanford University psychologist found that people who believe their abilities can expand over time, those with a "growth mind set," are the most innovative.[1]

They believe they can increase their abilities if they try and are willing to seek new strategies rather than succumb to fears of failure. Such openness is an attitude this book can help you develop, if you don't have it already.

But maintaining a constant growth mind set is not automatic. Whether or not you do, there is almost always a new challenge that may make you feel unready, unsteady, or inadequate. At such points, perhaps start by acting as if you are ready to proceed. That attitude may be your starter yeast for growth.

## Create your future

You already know how challenging it is to foretell the future. Consistent control and orderliness are just not in the cards, especially in the very situations that offer opportunity and flexibility. Then perhaps "the best way to predict the future is to create it," attributed to both Abraham Lincoln and management guru Peter Drucker.

*Choose Courage* contributes to building your resilience by helping you prepare for what's possible and pertinent to address in our dynamic worlds. Then you'll feel somewhat ready for external changes that can affect your life, even though all of them cannot be anticipated.

Move from reacting to considering your needs, addressing them, and asserting yourself as possible. That will help you become better ready to make choices in your interest and to take

17

action. Though one person's influence may seem minimal, who knows what effect a subtle movement or presence may have. Coined by American mathematician and meteorologist Edward Lorenz as the butterfly effect, this idea of a small action prompting big change is captured in <u>chaos theory</u>. An example from your own life may come to mind when you remember how someone's concrete encouragement empowered you.

In case you're not convinced of the complexity and challenges of the future — and the opportunities they hold — examples of the many possible influences on and in your life are provided below. They include national trends, current quality of life issues, and matters directly related to your personal and professional life.

Despite the natural interaction and connections among the examples, they are organized into sections and subsections for ease of digestion and possible use. You may skim them for general ideas, flagging areas that interest you. If you want to dig a little deeper, consider doing any of the following.

- Modify and improve examples to suit yourself.

- Add your own examples and ideas in the spaces provided at the end of each part.

- Choose a few examples that you have the time and interest to explore and possibly address.

*Note*: Significant international issues such as climate change, trade, political conflict, and economic instability are not addressed. Focus on such complex, major issues now could distract from thinking about choices you may have from just staying informed to taking action within your world.

Though the numbers of examples may seem daunting, they are offered so you can see current realities and where you might want to invest your time, energy, and other resources. Just being aware of their complexity and interaction may provide context for your own situation. At least, awareness will help you be prepared for harsh surprises. At best, perhaps opportunities for action to benefit yourself in work and life will emerge in your mind and in reality.

When you note the relationships among relevant factors in your life, maybe you'll see opportunities for two-fors, or seeing how dealing with one matter may promote a better result in another. As appropriate, start from where you are: your knowledge, interests, and connections. That will help avoid detours into overly ambitious efforts that could gobble time and energy without showing some satisfying outcomes.

To make the most of the experience, best skim the examples when you're in a mild, curious mood. Imagine you're on a voyage of possibilities rather than having to actually deal immediately with any of the realities mentioned. Instead, just flag any you may imagine exploring sometime in the future. Throughout this Step, you'll find some guidance for manageable action to benefit your current situation.

# General national trends, tendencies, and influences

General national trends can affect your economic, social, and political situation, as well as resources and options. The examples below are divided into subcategories to ease review. Nevertheless, you'll see overlapping and intermingling as is natural in much of life.

Of course, you cannot change these trends, tendencies, and influences. But you may have some opportunities to influence them through your work, resources, contacts, or persona. Or you could become curious about some related situations and choices as you consider them.

However close or distant these realities seem, you may decide to stay at least somewhat informed about any that could affect your life and people you cherish. That alertness could lessen discomfort, anxiety, fear, or possibly suffering, as well as help with decision making.

When a matter is important to you and possible to address, express your concerns and interests to individuals, groups, and organizations that can do something about it.   To get better attention, develop new relationships and build on current ones. Demonstrating   common   or   complementary   interests   can strengthen such outreach.

Possibly connect with elected representatives as well as others with resources and authority. If interested, form a community action group using current affiliations, work through your professional contacts, or imagine other ways you want to make a difference.

For example, you might take a few steps to green your home or to organize neighbors to work together on a small project. Maybe form a group to conserve resources at work or your house of worship. Use public transportation and bicycles, as possible.

As you skim the summaries of trends, tendencies, and influences below, feel free to skip all that seem irrelevant or too far removed from your life.

Recognizing that any one of the following economic matters could be worthy of a college course, choose or adapt one, if you wish. Criteria for choice might be that the example affects you life and learning about it would be important and interesting.

*Economic matters*

- possible increase in frequency, complexity, or depth of economic crises

- exposure to global economic forces and shifts as they directly affect your situation
- influence of corporate and union interests on policy, politics, and resource use
- changes in workforce size, skills, and composition
- mismatch of skills and organizational needs
- women over 60 making up the fastest growing segment of the workforce
- availability of public transportation
- tax reform
- regulations permitting many corporations to avoid paying taxes
- relation of lower savings patterns to longer-term economic security
- long-term unemployment
- distortions in income distribution
- about $150 billion annually spent on direct medical costs for debilitating mental illnesses
- increasing college costs mitigated by free online courses (MOOCs)
- _____
- _____

The following norms and behaviors could suggest areas to learn about, be alert to, or to enrich your life. Choose one for follow up , if you wish.

*Norms and behaviors*

- sexually active youngsters, teenagers, and older people

- increase in frequency of sexually transmitted diseases

- use of online dating sites

- participation in social networking sites, including sharing personal information among many people

- use of online purchasing services

- significant increase of and dependence on mobile phone use

- divorce rates of over 50% for first time marriages

- high illegitimacy rates (from 2% in 1940 to 40% in 2013)

- tensions between same-sex marriage and traditional marriage proponents

- continuation of work past conventional retirement age

- nearly four in ten families with children under 18 headed by women who are sole or primary breadwinners

- _____

- _____

How do any of the following demographic and social factors affect your life or community? Name one you can imagine addressing or learning about to benefit yourself and possibly others.

*Demographic and social matters*

- ethnic and religious groups with relatively high or low birth rates

- aging of the baby boomers

- improving life expectancy

- increased suicide rates for boomers and military members

- large numbers of wounded veterans from Iraq and Afghanistan wars

- disparate incarceration rates, large prison population, and recidivism issues

- approximately even number of households of singles and family units

© *Photograph by Andrew Winter*

## How will you and people you care about create meaning in later life?

- stay-at-home dads

- dual-career couples

- marriage and childbearing later in life

- high school graduation rate approaching highest in 40 years (75%)

- current college dropout rates highest in industrialized world

- _____

- _____

How may any of the following factors affect the health situation of yourself, family, and community? Where do you see an opportunity for improvement that you could influence?

*Health matters*

- increases of numbers of children with autism and of seniors with Alzheimer's disease

- integration of traditional and alternative (complementary) health care

- use of behavioral medicine to improve services and outcomes, and to lower costs

- lack of research, knowledge, and practice leading to appropriate adjustments of medicines and treatments based on unique recipient needs

- prevalence of AIDS among older people, women, African-Americans, and Hispanics

- shortages of nurses, allied health professionals, and medical generalists such as internists, pediatricians, and geriatricians

- higher medical costs largely due to fee-for-service approach as well as patient insurance practices, technology, increased as use of visits and medicines, demographic changes, malpractice insurance costs, and incentive structures

- lack of coordination of information and services as well as decision making among specialists and generalists, medical and dental providers

- variations in medical and dental treatment by ethnic group, age, and geographic area

- safety of service delivery involving emergency transportation, hospitals, and technology

- variations and changes in health care coverage and arrangements; education about and effective implementation of the Affordable Care Act

- estimated 11.5 million adults with a debilitating mental illness

- _____

- _____

Drawing the line between public safety and health matters is difficult. For example, drug and alcohol abuse can be included in either one. Which one of the following public safety points would warrant your attention?

*Public safety matters*

- effects of terrorist threats and actions on public safety and civil liberties

- obsolete, incompatible equipment and coordination challenges of first responders

- infrastructure degradation (e.g. roads, highways, levees, sewer systems, bridges, dams, water systems, and electrical power grids)

- inattention to dangers and prevention of accidents related to extracting and using natural resources, as well as avoiding repetition of previous problems with coal, oil, natural gas, and nuclear power

- drug and alcohol abuse
- availability of nuclear, biological, electro-magnetic pulse, chemicals, and other weapons of mass destruction to a range of dangerous sources

- _____

- _____

As a prelude to the next sections related to government matters, certainly interest groups and political parties have significant impact, as you know. How government works effectively, and not, can reflect the complex, interactive influences among the related lists below. Where might you want to contribute or make a difference?

*Political and other interest groups*

- fundamentalist groups within and outside religions
- lack of collaboration for and commitment to longer-term, general public welfare

- power of lobbying and advocacy groups to change government decision making and oversight (e.g. abortion rights, right to life, animal rights, gun ownership, particular business, financial, and union interests)

© *1995. Cartoon by Ruth M. Schimel*

- influence of bundlers of financial contributions and commentators at the extremes of left and right

- effects of drawing boundaries of electoral districts to suit political party and other interests

- narrow political motivations prevailing over effective policies to benefit wider populations

- lack of political majorities and consensus to focus outcomes benefitting the greater good

- _____

- _____

Using the three branches of government at the end of this section assists with focus, but doesn't reflect the interactive, overarching nature of realities as much as the following:

*Governmental matters*

   *General, especially interactive aspects*

- organization of legislative work and executive departments into silos of sometimes repetitive subjects, reflecting political fiefdoms and interest groups

- overlapping agencies and programs with vested interests in sustaining themselves

- lack of long-term vision and processes for anticipating problems and taking proactive, integrated action

- hard to understand, important issues that make effective management and public support difficult to marshal

- decrease of government resources and support for social and education programs at federal, state, and local levels

- viability of government-supported insurance programs such as Disability, Medicare, Medicaid, Unemployment Insurance, and, in the longer run, Social Security

- disrupted federal budget process

- public debt and deficits

- organizational blocks to addressing important long-term issues and opportunities related to energy sources, viability of electric grids, cyber security, quality of education, climate change, asymmetrical warfare, pension sustainability, and health care incentives, among other matters

- tendency to organize for and react to last disaster or problem rather than plan for a possibly different future one

- imbalance in use of resources for waging war, resolving conflict, and avoiding conflict

- _____
- _____

© *Photograph by Andrew Winter*

## *Continuing conflict and mutual destruction 'twas ever thus.*

*Legislative branch*

- cyberspace vulnerabilities: oversight, and protection

- increasing amounts of money and time used for campaigning and funding, distracting representatives from the people's business

- difficulty in creating effective consensus for promoting balanced, responsible outcomes

- overlapping, conflicting constituencies and committee structure

- infiltration and influence of special interests on development of regulations

- ineffective anticipation and protection of the public from speculation and financial schemes that benefit the few (e.g. mortgage lending practices, irresponsible leveraging by banks and other financial entities)

- blockage of judicial nominations

- _____

- _____

*Executive branch*

- enforcement of product and service standards for imports as well as domestic sources

- problematic policy implementation exacerbated by overlap, conflict, competition, and inadequate coordination of resources by federal, state, and local governments

- large proportion of contractors doing government work; difficulty of ensuring effective oversight and limitation

- government by executive order to circumvent legislative blocks

- rigid, time-consuming employment processes and practices

- difficulty of doing effective performance evaluation, based on specific criteria

- numbers of knowledgeable, experienced workers slated to retire

- complex, time-consuming regulations that inhibit effectiveness of businesses especially and their competitiveness abroad

- _____

- _____

*Judicial branch*

- significant Supreme Court and lower court decisions reflecting ideological predilections
- interpretations of legislative and regulatory intentions that affect subsequent implementation
- length of time for cases to be processed and ultimately decided
- fewer numbers of judges available to do increasing work, in part due to legislative holdups
- _____
- _____

Though you may not have the power, interest, or resources to change or influence any of the foregoing, your choices about how you keep informed, prepare, and live could make a difference for yourself and others in your communities.

Following are matters more likely to affect you directly.

# Current quality of life issues

*Environment*
- indoor and outdoor air pollution
- reliable sanitary water delivery and waste removal systems
- availability of inexpensive, uninterrupted electricity
- severe weather
- local capacities to deal with results of natural disasters, including coordination and communication issues
- limits on and cost of natural resources such as oil and water

© *Photograph by Amé Solomon*

## Some generational views of resource use

- _____

- _____

*Health and safety*

- access to appropriate medical and dental services and their insurance coverage

- public safety coordination within the community

- neighborhood demographic shifts and maintenance

- food safety
- availability and cost of nutritionally beneficial food
- _____
- _____

*Economic matters*

- consistent availability, cost, and security of technical means of communication such as computers, Internet, Web sites, mobile phones, landlines, social networking processes, and combinations
- state of local economy
- identity theft
- transportation and travel difficulties, including regularity, safety, costs, congestion, and quality of services
- quality of consumer services and protection from exploitation
- fluctuation of local real estate values
- _____
- _____

Whether or not you have the resources and time to make a difference you'd want, your optimism, due diligence, and organized actions may be influential in regard to the foregoing.

The examples below are most likely to affect your life directly now. They provide more accessible opportunities for choice and action.

# Personal and professional choices for immediate attention

*Work and economic matters*

- employment security and stability
- financial security
- retirement resources
- work identity and role changes
- personal debt
- location and environment of work
- meaning and satisfaction
- opportunities for advancement, including leadership and management
- professional relationships and connections that support goals
- _____
- _____

*Training and education*

- schooling and education levels commensurate with ambitions
- periodic renewal of skills, expansion of capacities, and refreshed focus
- effective, continuing education and training related to future opportunities
- _____
- _____

*Family, including extended and family-by-choice connections*

- family stability
- intergenerational responsibilities
- living arrangements

- child care
- location and environment of home
- quality of intimate relationships
- _____
- _____

*Healthy habits*

- habits supporting physical and mental health, related to yourself and people you cherish
- natural, healthy process of aging
- effective, routine health care: preventive, integrated, and reactive
- _____
- _____

*Personal relationships and community*

- satisfying, close relationships that have meaning to you
- friends and other loved ones who are enjoyable, stimulating, and supportive
- spiritual and religious community involvements
- _____
- _____

# Deciding what you want to do about influences on your situation

The full picture of the considerations above and immediate influences on your life, as well as any you've added in the spaces provided, may give you pause, if not indigestion! Maybe it's a miracle that things are as manageable as they are, especially when you deal with them based on priorities and what you can actually do.

Nevertheless, some jeopardy, negative stress, and certainly challenge exist for many people in one form or another. Since your power comes primarily from within, attending to where your choices lie may at least help you anticipate and deal better with your situation and realities you consider important.

Starting within yourself, use the following ideas about good stress to strengthen your hand. Studies of stress hark back at least to Hans Selye's 1974 book, *Stress without Distress*. Later research found that certain attitudes provide protection from bad stress which contributes to illnesses, mental as well as physical, and their interactions. Since wishing won't make it so, how would you adopt or adapt these three views related to good stress to benefit yourself?

- belief that you have control or influence over situations and events in your life

- commitment or the ability to feel deeply involved in your activities

- anticipation of change as an exciting challenge for further development[2]

You may see value in these views and want to strengthen them in yourself. If so, suggestions for getting ready to access your courage in Step Two and other parts of this book can help.

Making modifications or change work for you will also contribute. Start by focusing as much as possible, devoting energies and time to what you *want* to and *can* do. For instance, they may include any of the following:

- development efforts related to work and personal life

- participation in political, spiritual, or community groups

- regular time for pleasure and renewal

- work projects that have meaning to you.

Possibly experiment with the following suggestions to set your priorities for action. Refer back to the three previous lists of trends, influences on quality of life, and personal and professional choices as well as your additions in the blank spaces at the end of each one:

- Check all that you can influence you directly. Among your choices, circle only the checks for matters you truly can and want to influence.

- For the ones you checked and circled, choose the top five likely to improve quality of life now for you and the people you cherish.

- Focus your efforts on the most beneficial, engaging, and manageable one first, returning to the others as you wish.

## Clarifying and moving forward with your first choice

Let's say you selected "periodic renewal of skills, expansion of capacities, and refreshed focus" from in the training and education list above. Perhaps when you first consider this category or any other you prefer, you're not sure of where to start.

To make the process digestible, carve out one manageable part. Perhaps choose a skill or ability you'd really enjoy using, can develop now, and have the resources to proceed. Should nothing come to mind immediately, wait a day or so. Then re-visit your choice to see what ideas and images emerge.

If you still draw a blank, just keep returning about once a week until a subject or some simple ideas to explore ignite your interest enough to act. You may also engage a few people you respect and trust in conversation about possibilities; offer to assist them with something they're looking into, if that seems appropriate.

Avoid giving or eliciting advice from others. Instead, keep an open mind using a form of brainstorming such as:

- Let participants' imaginations play with any possibility, jotting down the basic points for all to see and discuss.

- Find patterns among those points, including identification of one action that could contribute to more than one goal.

- Choose the most appealing, viable action you can, scheduling a start date within a week.

For a more complex situation or goal, try or adapt the brainstorming process above as well as any of the following:

- Discuss your ideas with a few of your possible collaborators after doing some sleuthing on your own to learn basic aspects.

- Have conversations about related subjects with some resourceful and open-minded friends, family members, mentors, and colleagues.

When you're ready to proceed with a relatively simple or more complex vision, use any of the following questions to help focus and organize your approach:

- Identify how you learn best and apply what you select in the actions you take. For example, do you learn best by listening, reading, watching, interviewing, writing, sketching, practicing, doing, or some combination?

- What one or two formal and informal opportunities for learning and action will you create or use?

- What concrete, manageable goal will you describe for yourself now? Create a viable time line. Start by scheduling at least one modest action each week.

- How will you define progress?

- What will you do to acknowledge any assistance you receive as well as your own accomplishments?

Decide how long is reasonable to work on any choice you make, allotting necessary time and resources during that period. With each modest effort, keep rewarding yourself along the way with positive reinforcement. To determine this, ask yourself what will bring you pleasure or satisfaction that's healthy, accessible, and safe?

In addition, simple gifts to yourself for self-renewal may include:

- taking time for walks, reading for pleasure, or listening to music

- engaging in lively conversations with people who interest you

- entertaining and stimulating yourself by watching videos and TV

- allotting regular times for solitude and personal attention

When you don't accomplish what you want, avoid blame. Instead, ask yourself what's holding you back and how you can apply what your response tells you. Then start again with a more focused, small step.

Or let go of the idea or activity if it no longer fits you or your goals well after some initial experiences and conversation with yourself. For example, why continue reading, or even skimming a book or article that you don't find useful or engaging? On a more significant level, why remain part of something that harms, wastes time and resources, or holds you back? Among other things, that could relate to relationships, groups, activities, and work projects where you have some choice.

Or put your decision aside for a specific period of time until the situation improves or you see a better way through. Just don't keep repeating the same behaviors and wondering why things haven't improved.

Whatever you commit to, don't expect linear, consistent progress. Being willing in itself will not lead to action that entirely erases barriers and blocks. In addition to your own efforts, engage your collaborators to discuss ways to work through and around them. To assist, explore the ideas and actions suggested in Steps Three and Four related to negative emotions and habits that hold you back. Continue celebrating all efforts and outcomes you value, no matter how modest.

## Using the tension between stability and change

Gain some comfort and sustenance from the information you've developed about your areas for action and the small steps involved suggested here or developed yourself. Even the most modest outcomes from what you're doing accrue and ultimately contribute to your progress. In contrast, the "big bangs" can be quickly over, soon fading from memory. Often, what gives more lasting pleasure and meaning is how your efforts come together over time, the experiences you have along the way on your own and with others.

Expect that the process of living will usually bring tensions. By embracing them, you'll likely be stretching yourself from your comfort zone to an improved perch. That's what tension literally means — to stretch.

Will you go through the discomfort, anxiety, pain, or suffering or avoid them and remain static? Or even regress? Winds and waves may buffet, yet you'll weather them.

Consider your own experience in choosing what to do, then. You already know from your past that most worthwhile activities will be challenging. In fact, brains and bodies are designed to learn and develop. They remain receptive during almost all ages and conditions. In contrast, automatic repetition is likely to lead to tennis elbow of the mind — not just of the elbow.

© *Photograph by Andrew Winter*

### *Winds will blow and pass, especially as you choose safer situations.*

If you decide to continue moving forward, remind yourself of how you've dealt successfully with previous challenges and explorations. What comes to mind when you think about:

- specific things you did and how you did them

- positive emotions that charged your motivation

- who helped you do well

- what you've learned that's relevant from the clues in others' struggles in stories you heard, shared, or read, personal vignettes, articles, and biographies?

## Your struggles are natural and likely as "old" as time itself

Maybe these reminders from the Bible will help you see how long such classic, creative struggles have been going on. *Ecclesiastes* in the Old Testament captures the natural tension between stability and change as well as the paradoxes of living.

At a general level, "What has been is what will be, and what has been done is what will be done; and there is nothing new under the sun." On the individual level, "There is nothing better for a man than he should eat and drink, and find enjoyment in his toil." Instead of the repetition implied in the first quotation, imagine the sustenance and pleasant stretch available in the second.

If, as *Ecclesiastes* also says, "two are better than one" and "a dream comes with much business," your relationships and vision for the future contribute to the stretching process. Imbedded in your past are hints of what is to come and experience that shows the way forward, or at least what to avoid.

Add to your knowledge and experience by using your intuition to know when and how to proceed, what to reject and embrace. Alternatively, sometimes it's just best to practice a little, possibly with some assistance, before jumping into the pool without knowing how to swim – or at least float.

Consider the following excerpt from *Ecclesiastes* as possible metaphors in your life, rather than just taking it literally.

> *For everything there is a season, and a time for every matter under heaven:*
> *a time to be born, and a time to die;*
> *a time to plant, and a time to pluck up what is planted;*
> *a time to kill, and a time to heal;*
> *a time to break down, and a time to build up;*
> *a time to weep, and a time to laugh;*
> *a time to mourn, and a time to dance;*
> *a time to cast away stones, and a time to gather stones together;*
> *a time to embrace, and a time to refrain from embracing;*
> *a time to seek, and a time to lose;*
> *a time to keep, and a time to cast away;*
> *a time to rend, and a time to sew;*
> *a time to keep silence, and a time to speak;*
> *a time to love, and a time to hate;*
> *a time for war, and a time for peace.*

Given the complexity of what unfolds in most lives, I'd be surprised if your choices will be this clear. You probably won't have time for even one important activity; boundaries will not be clean or simple. Instead, imagine along with poet Yehudah Amichai in "A Man in His Life," changing gender references as you wish:

> *A man needs to love and to hate at the same moment,*
> *to laugh and cry with the same eyes,*
> *with the same hands to throw stones and to gather them,*
> *to make love in war and war in love.*
> *And to hate and forgive and remember and forget,*
> *to arrange and confuse, to eat and digest*
> *what history takes years and years to do.*

Notice how Amichai uses that small, but critical, word *and* throughout his poem. You may "hate *and* forgive or remember *and* forget" or "laugh *and* cry, "pretty much all at once. Ever see, for example, how the facial expressions for the latter two seem similar? Maybe they're not so different fundamentally.

His poem captures the complex opportunities of living. For example, how can you be independent and collaborative? Perhaps bring your original ideas to an interested team. Or be responsible and experimental? Perhaps, do simple, effective planning for new approaches; engage people who can complement your strengths.

How else can you play with building bridges using *ands?* For example, can you work hard and take time off? Maybe seriously commit to learning a new sport through which the effort elicits endorphins that relax you?

Whether or not your combinations of actions seem logical, try to see what's possible, useful, and engaging. Your authentic, heartfelt ways of working things through, or *how* you proceed, can be as catalytic as *what* you actually do.

Remember, for example, the seeming mess when you first tried to organize a huge amount of stuff or information. Or your emotions whenever you started something new and challenging. You may feel confused or overwhelmed, even when you have a plan of action.

One way to start is to identify the basics, just what you need to know and do to get started. Get assistance or collaborate with people you like and respect. Remind yourself of how you've used your patience and humor in the past. Continue toward your goal with small, regular steps, maybe devoting about an hour every day or so. Adjust your plan as needed to lessen the mess and move toward relative order — until you and your complex life unravel into temporary confusion again, of course.

Throughout the process, avoid over thinking what you plan to do or postponing action. Instead take modest, manageable steps that honor who you are and what you want, with time out for rest and fun. Avoid perseverating about what you're NOT doing. To spark energy to continue a pleasant rhythm of action, keep a list of to-dos, maybe three to five daily, so you won't have to keep revisiting requirements.

Finally, be open to your intuition and emotions, sources of energy and motivation. For variety, explore some new or different ideas, people, and situations. To encourage yourself, name one you'd like to learn about within the next week. Schedule an hour or so by blocking time on your calendar.

Certainly not all change, even what you influence, brings progress. But whatever the outcome, at least you won't regret responsible, apt effort. More likely, though, your wholehearted participation in processes you choose will eventually bring many of the benefits you seek and perhaps some sweet surprises.

By appreciating the rich and sometimes frustrating paradoxes that often come with worthwhile situations, you'll be more likely to promote good outcomes. Again, using the word *and* extends possibilities. Ask yourself, how can I attend to both resentments *and* love of the same person, without letting the former cloud the latter? Another approach is to be persistent about your passion and passionate about your persistence.

## Taking steps now

I hope you'll find at least one idea for responsible action that is enjoyable and productive from the material you've just read and considered so far. To encourage yourself further, translate any of the related, general suggestions below into one step you will take to improve your current situation:

- Explore, enjoy, or build on one aspect of your current situation that's promising within the next two days.

- Figure out one way to make a small change in your life work in your favor.

- Accept the disappointments, frustrations, and sorrows that go with being alive. How might you minimize one that's particularly significant now?

- Learn from and apply one insight from a mistake or regret, rather than dwell on it.

- Spend time regularly and possibly collaborate with one or two people you enjoy and respect.

## Bottom line

Whether internal or external, an impending or actual shift or change can provoke discomfort, anxiety, fear, or even suffering. Staying stuck in such emotions, remaining just an observer, or avoiding opportunities can keep you and your courage in escrow. So *do bother* in order to influence, benefit from, and enjoy what life offers you and others. Remind yourself of your capacity for courage as you remember the new definition based on my original research.

Courage is a process of becoming involving:

- *the willingness to realize your true capacities*

- *by going **through** discomfort, fear, anxiety, or suffering*

- *and taking wholehearted, responsible action.*

# STEP TWO:
# Getting Ready to Express Your Courage

## First, It Is All About You

*Whatever I own is temporary, since we're only here for a short period of time. It's what we do and produce; it's our actions that will last forever. That's real value.*

Billionaire, Nicholas Berggruen

*Becoming courageous involves the willingness to realize your true capacities by going* **through** *discomfort, fear, anxiety, or suffering and taking wholehearted, responsible action.*

Definition of the process of becoming courageous from Ruth Schimel's dissertation research

I've long been intrigued by what leads people, including myself, to move from thinking, feeling, and talking to acting in their interests. My father, the teacher and engineer said, "Readiness is all." Shakespeare said it too, but Pop may not have known that.

My question to him still needs an answer: "How do you get ready?"

This Step offers an approach that recognizes getting ready does not happen overnight, especially when interests are authentic and goals are significant. Nor is the process linear or logical much of the time. With these realities in mind, invoke your potential by taking modest, rhythmic steps for your benefit.

To honor who you are and who you want to be, four ways to choose courage are offered below. They relate to your authenticity, commitment, passions, and vocation.

## Realizing Your True Self: Authenticity

> *Be yourself. Everyone else is taken.*
> Irish writer and poet, Oscar Wilde

As you have already seen, expressing your true self is a continuing process starting even before self-awareness. For example, have you noticed how personalities of most babies appear very early, especially as they act spontaneously in their world?

**Little boy playing in front of the camera.**

Then, the first decade or so seems to be about socialization: how children are molded to fit in or how they rebel, both influenced by others. Perhaps much of the rest of life can be considered a process of trying to return to that original self at a more evolved level. The tension for many individuals is how to approximate right proportion between conformity and independence.

In other words, answers to the question, "Who am I?" are dynamic as well as grounded. You reflect your nature *and* nurture.

Physiologically, behavior is also influenced by epigenetics, factors that cause your genes to "express themselves" differently. They intertwine in complex ways.

Also contributing to appreciating our complexity are recent explorations of friendly bacteria, the micro biota discussed in Michael Pollan's 2013 article, *Some of My Best Friends Are Germs:* *http://www.nytimes.com/2013/05/19/magazine/say-hello-to-the-100-trillion-bacteria-that-make-up-your-microbiome.html?ref=magazine&_r=0* . If you think the 26,000 to more than 150,000 genes are significant, imagine the influence of the 100 trillion bacteria and their genes on your body. And this is just your biology.

But your genes or your bacteria's genes can't make you do anything. That would cede your power to biology alone. While physical influences are certainly important, the focus in *Choose Courage* is on how you decide and act to realize your true capacities.

To imagine your focus, picture yourself as a sun, a core of energy that holds essential aspects of your identity in a mighty roil. You are an ever-shifting system of relationships, cycles, and varying environments held in creative tension by your nature, perceptions, and actions.

## Using your own center to sustain and create stability

As change occurs, clarity, and confidence about your core self can provide some predictability and reassurance. Though shifts in expression emerge with learning, time, and experience, these are many of the factors that contribute to your core or essence:

- genetic predispositions

- values

- self-awareness and appreciation

- early childhood influences

- learned skills, knowledge, and abilities that you value

- intuition and instinct

- intellect

- interests and passions

- lessons from mistakes and detours

- temperament

- physical appearance and capacities

To appreciate yourself more fully, take about five minutes to tease out a few key words and short descriptions related to any one of the categories above. Without over thinking, jot down quickly several positive words or phrases that come to mind about how you express the one you chose.

If you want to try this process with any of the other factors, now or later, feel free to do so. That exploration can provide some concreteness for appreciating your core. As author Anais Nin said, "There are few human beings who receive the truth complete and staggering by instant illumination. Most of them acquire it fragment by fragment, on a small scale, by successive developments, like a mosaic."

In keeping with this reality, consider enriching your views of yourself later by exchanging positive, specific descriptions with others. Choose people you trust and respect who know you well in at least one aspect of your life. Make sure they and you are not pushing a conscious or unconscious agenda, however well-meaning. When you want to explore more deeply, use information you develop elsewhere in *Choose Courage* as well as insights that continue to emerge over time.

Although you may have been imprinted by early relationships and experiences, as an adult you now have choices about how to live and express yourself. But let's face it. Few people are totally free agents. Situations, other people, and hangovers from the past influence you. Current responsibilities and demands intrude. In fact, recent research on social networks shows[3] how other people continue to affect behavior, even including habits related to eating and smoking.

By noticing how you relate to others, you may see where you tend to perch along the line between conformity or accommodation on one end and independence or authenticity on the other. You can get ideas about such tendencies by watching how children, teenagers, and adults relate to one another. What behaviors have you observed in others?

How much of your own dress, communication patterns, mannerisms, and habits continue to reflect such tendencies? More importantly, how would you want to re-visit and modify deeper aspects of yourself that reflect early or current influences that no longer benefit you? Identify just one example from the following categories and any others that come to mind:

- values and beliefs
- behavior in relationships
- work choices
- attitudes toward.....

- expectations about ......

- use of time

- ambition

- sense of humor

- openness toward others and new possibilities

To address a tendency toward conformity or independence you may want to modify, what one, specific, modest action makes sense for you to take within the next few days or during an expected situation? How would it express your true self and what you want in life? Imagine how you'd proceed. When and how will you try out your idea?

Awareness of where you're comfortable along the continuum between conformity and authenticity or accommodation and independence may help expand your repertoire of options. If you tend toward conformity, how might you want to let go of one aspect of the roles and habits that don't reflect your current self or who you want to be? On the other hand, name one or two situations where some conformity would be productive or apt.

Your actual power emerges more freely when choices reflect your authentic, core self. Though you have little control of others, you may influence them. Generally, you have even less control of your environment.

Of course there is some risk when you open the doors to dynamic realities: your core self, relationships, and environment. You can't predict how things will work out. But what seems unknown is often where much of the adventure and possibilities of life could reside.

*Dangers of Being True to Yourself*
by Ruth M. Schimel
*(with apologies to Elizabeth Barrett Browning)*

*Pushed by the murmurings of what you should do, would do,
and won't do because someone said to,
Let's count the ways you put your true self in danger:*

*Listening uncritically to echoes of the departed,
Brings the hangover of who they wanted you to be, what they
believe you should do.*

*Wanting to please the living,
Brings specious success that meets just their needs.*

*Trying to fit an image of what a good girl or boy you are,
Brings the ballast of beliefs other than yours.*

*Feeling regret at not fulfilling that endless list of what you
have to do,
Brings impossible expectations that generate guilt.*

*Doing the opposite of what others dictate,
Makes real choice no longer yours.*

*Wanting to parade the looks and labels that impress others,
Brings just a pass to their world.*

*Avoiding what you can do for yourself,
Leads to stasis, boredom, and dependency.*

*Beware tyrannies of shoulds and regrets about might-have-beens:*
*Instead, choose ways to thwart these dangers.*

*Name your traps.*
*Avoid them, finding humor in such situations whenever possible.*
*If you can't, at least loosen their knots so you can wiggle out.*

*And then,*
*Strive to be true to who you are,*
*Do well and good, thriving along the way,*
*while embracing the messy process of living.*

## What may happen as you strive to be who you are

Despite awareness of who you want to be and what may be keeping you from it, understanding everything all at once and being able to take effective action are unlikely. Even when you are at a high level of self-knowledge, you are in process with others and your environment. Situations shift. Needs are almost met, yet would still benefit from further attention.

You often have something better in mind. Or as philosopher Martin Heidegger said, "My self is always my openness and involvement with being in the world."[4]

Then one way of nurturing and refining your true self is to be open or revealed, within a zone of safety you create or choose. In other words, if no one is privy to who you truly are, what benefit do you and others get from your being in the world?

## Will you just cast a shadow, or emerge more clearly and directly?

If you accept the common sense of these questions about your possible impact, at least one other person has to be present for you to be heard and probably to hear yourself clearly. People of good intention can then become interested in and appreciate you. They are more likely to provide satisfying support and assistance because you have let them see you. In turn, you are encouraged to be open with and responsive to them. Cycles of mutual appreciation and trust are then likely to develop, however spasmodically.

As boundaries between yourself and others become more permeable, you all become more apparent. Although there's some risk that the influence of others could possibly dilute your core tendencies, there are benefits as well.

© *Photograph by Andrew Winter*

### *Will you just cast a shadow, or emerge more clearly and directly?*

You move from reacting to hearing your true self through accurate feedback, from only pleasing yourself or others to finding grounds for mutual, beneficial accommodation. Over time, the ease that comes with relaxing vigilance grows further. The process supports building satisfying relationships that are sustainable and strong as well as more enjoyable.

To the person who is used to the security of roles with clear boundaries – or anyone for that matter – this process of self-discovery through openness naturally creates some sense of vulnerability. Even appropriate openness can sometimes feel like emptying oneself or over-exposure.

To avoid or move beyond this, shift behaviors gently. Initially and even during the process, expect some discomfort or anxiety because you will not be able to predict entirely what will emerge from within yourself nor others' responses. All the better possibilities for variety and adventure, though.

To be alert to hideouts from being apparent, here are examples of limiting roles you may want to adjust or influence:

- martyr mother, father, friend, sibling, or colleague who may make others feel guilty because they don't measure up

- family member or other close person devoted primarily to climbing the career ladder or chasing the next deal

- accommodator, concerned with pleasing others at the expense of making authentic, reasonable requests, also known as the compliant one

- avoider of responsibility, waiting to be rescued

- controller

- competitive sibling or colleague

58

© *Photograph by Andrew Winter*

### *Walk the labyrinths of life to see where they take you and how you want to move beyond their boundaries.*

Modifying and letting go of limiting roles and willingness to be open can improve experiences and relationships. In fact, your changing behavior may help others consider how they may be stuck in confining roles.

Being genuine stimulates a positive cycle of naturalness, also supporting ease and comfort. Time and energy wasted in inauthentic role playing and other detours from being true to oneself can then be redirected for enjoying life and reaching out to new people and groups.

The likely challenge of exploring and testing the waters with different social networks feels more like fun than threat.[5] As your repertoire of behaviors also expands, you'll find increased options for action and variety.

Relaxing into being your fuller self, helps you increase receptivity to others. That process also contributes to being aware of whatever behaviors work for you and with people who are important to you. Combine your intention or choice and will to grow, as psychologist Rollo May might say.[6]   In other words, receptivity does not translate to reactive conformity, but to being available and accessible.

*Image is in the public domain believed to be free to use without restriction in the US.*

### *Choose your favorite pillow to support your comfort with authenticity.*

Between experiments with increased openness, you may sense some fuzziness. In not being able to predict how you will show up or how others will respond, you move into what feels like and certainly may be unknown territory. Not knowing what could be coming out of your protective chrysalis, you face the possible anxiety of feeling a stranger to yourself. This is a good time to get nourishment from revisiting the core self you explored at the start of this Step.

With each authentic action, you'll likely feel stronger, more curious about how things will work out, than anxious. You'll get positive results — or at least move beyond feeling stuck or static.

Maybe you'll look back on previous concerns and situations and wonder what the big deal was. You'll also see how something that seemed mysterious, unclear, difficult, or threatening is basically manageable. Even failures, mistakes, or misunderstandings you could be trying to avoid can be bridges to a better future, when understood, addressed, and moved across. Blunders have been known to be fertile ground for progress, in fact.

Throughout this process, your full self sharpens. By allowing the world in, you connect better with what's outside yourself. Over time, you participate more effectively with a wider range of communities of your choosing.

But you could also find danger. As Sergeant Phil Esterhaus used to say on the TV series *Hill Street Blues,* "Hey, let's be careful out there." In groups and organizations, interest in power and control can trump merit and value. In families, which also tend to be hierarchical, members may prefer the predictable status quo.

That specious comfort seems better than appreciating what you've become and could become, how habitual interpersonal dynamics limit most everyone involved. No matter how confident anyone seems, fears of change can prompt behaviors that serve neither them nor you.

So be prepared for a range of possibilities, from encouraging to discouraging, from safe to dangerous. Identify what you want to modify, what you can influence, and what you will let go. And by all means, continue to reward yourself for any progress in ways that have meaning to you.

## Choices

Actually you know and sense a great deal about how to serve your interests already. Taking action for good purpose is the continuing challenge.

Perhaps start by noting people who use you and others, those who take only.

What individuals, groups and situations are best avoided or kept at arm's length? To move forward, what one person, group, or role would you want to let go? What relationships do you want to modify now?

Also consider how you can find and connect with people and situations that welcome you as you are, to where you can be yourself. Use such havens for being authentic as islands of relative sanity and safety. They could already be available within your family, among your friends and colleagues, at work, in school, and in your communities. How might you create them, as well?

If these new situations aren't accessible now, at least work on improving important relationships you have already. What one or two actions will you take within the next week? Maybe work collaboratively on a continuing issue, give positive, specific feedback, or ask what you can do to help. Schedule one approach on your calendar to go beyond thinking to making palpable progress.

To expand possibilities, keep considering and cultivating less conventional connections such as families by choice as well as friends and colleagues with different views and experience. Among them, choose people you respect and enjoy who at least value your worth. The more authentic you become the greater influence you'll have on others. Instead of their "training" you to their ways, you will offer equally valid alternatives. Better this than reacting, feeling trapped in others' rituals, or being confined by limiting or exploitive situations.

Sometimes a metaphor can help ideas mesh. In this process of letting go and engaging freshly, imagine piloting a ship moving across a sea you've chosen to explore. Or maybe you'll be riding a surfboard. You're capable of flowing with the sometimes unpredictable elements while charting your own course. Although you're floating on something that can shift and even threaten to swallow, you have chosen your means of movement; you are original, self-contained, and separate while related to the world you're in. You remain at the helm of your ship of self — or at least know how to swim!

### *What surf do you want to ride? What waves and means appeal?*

Or, as Munro Leaf, the author of the children's book, *Ferdinand the Bull*, taught:

> Like the cowardly lion in the <u>Wizard of Oz</u>, *Ferdinand the Bull is not what others expect him to be...Every child knows what it is to be forced to do something that he or she just does not want to do. Another writer would have clumsily transformed timid Ferdinand into a hero of the bullring. But Leaf knew that true courage is being true to one's self. No matter what anyone else might say. And it is within himself that Ferdinand finds true happiness.*[7]

## Practices for Realizing Your True Self

Try any one or combine aspects of the following three approaches that appeal. Make sure to adjust your choices and actions to what promises to work well for you and is worth your time.

**1. *Identify and use specific words and themes to guide choices for action:*** Describe your preferences by jotting down five or so of your own key words and phrases related to each of the important aspects of your life below. Avoid over thinking this process, choosing your first reactions and listening to your intuition. Also avoid relying primarily on the examples provided; that may distract from your natural inclinations.

***Relationships:*** (examples: intimate, friendly, honest, reserved, open, enhancing, fun, warm, mutual, balanced, stimulating, beneficial, imaginative)

***Work:*** including for pay, volunteer, at home: (examples: fair recompense, good match, flexible, promising, worthwhile, high-paying, prestigious, secure, creative, challenging, interesting, useful, productive, enjoyable, innovative)

***Play:*** (examples: organized, demanding, spontaneous, fun, vigorous, relaxing, social, solitary, exciting, healthy, and creative)

- What common themes do you notice among the words and phrases you choose, from among the examples and your own?

- Put the top three for each category in priority order, using them as criteria to guide your decisions and actions for a while.

- Test their value as guides by seeing if the results of your choices improve the quality and pleasure of your life.

- Identify new descriptions as you move forward to reflect your initial progress and evolution.

**2. *Learn from issues:*** When you feel constrained, unhappy, or frustrated, write or record a description of your emotions in a short paragraph. Notice what specifically prompted them. Or use another form of art you'd like such as drawing, dancing, or singing. Make sure whatever form of expression you choose captures internal and external aspects of the matter. Avoid blaming others as well as yourself. If you wish, have a conversation about your insights with someone you trust who's also interested in exploring self-development.

What one action do the main themes suggest you take now? Once done, stay open to additional choices.

However you capture your insights and information using the means you select, periodically gather related information. See what ideas for action a continuing conversation with yourself about what you notice provokes. As possible, pick a viable one for follow up each time.

In addition to providing data for action and possibly opening new doors, this approach can also download your concerns. That could avoid cluttering your mind with self-chatter, repetitive thoughts, and over thinking, all often escapes from *doing* something. Continue staying alert for themes, insights, ideas, and inspirations that support your momentum, honoring any progress you make and learning from what's holding you back.

**3. *Pamper yourself:*** Name some enjoyable activities you can and want to do that reflect or express an authentic aspect of yourself. Schedule one a week, providing adequate time for follow through. Check any possibilities below that appeal and add your own.

### *Activities that don't cost anything except precious time:*
___ Listen to your favorite music on the radio, CDs, iPod, Pandora, or other sources.

___ Surf www.youtube.com for engaging videos.

___Read an interesting book, magazine, or article on hand or from the library.

___ Write something that expresses your true self such as phrases, paragraphs, or poetry.

___ Compose and send a thoughtful letter, text, note, or e-mail to someone who is important to you.

___Plan a special activity for yourself, gathering information from research, the Internet, friends, and materials at hand.

___ Take a walk or run in a peaceful area.

___ Spend time with a good friend doing whatever appeals to you both.

___ Go to a free exhibit or museum to see something that interests you or to just wander around.

___ Join a choir or other group that allows you to express an aspect of yourself.

___ Take a leisurely bath or swim.

___ Exchange appropriate massages with a loved one.

___ Attend a free lecture or presentation that explores a topic that intrigues you.

___ Take a walk and have a conversation with a child or an older person.

___ Hide or send surprise notes of affection.

___ Learn about body movement you might enjoy such as yoga, dance, and stretching.

___ Play a game that's fun with people you like.

___ Sit on a park bench, porch, or steps and observe what's there and happening.

___ Take a 20-30 minute nap when you feel tired.

___ Daydream and fantasize.

___ Have a good conversation with a stimulating person.

___ Go to a botanical garden or other public place of beauty.

___ Watch or participate in a community sport.

___ Exchange magazines and newspapers of interest with family, friends, and neighbors.

___ Practice a musical instrument you enjoy.

___ Sing in the shower.

___ Do nothing, just breathing deeply and letting thoughts emerge (or not).

## *Activities That May Cost Something:*

\_\_ Take a day off and do whatever strikes your fancy.

\_\_ Obtain a video that you'd want to see more than once or download one.

\_\_ Subscribe to a magazine or buy a book about a topic that interests you.

\_\_ Watch or participate in an entertaining movie or show.

\_\_ Buy clothes or accessories that express yourself.

\_\_ Take a class or workshop that gives you something tangible to take away and use.

\_\_ Explore appealing alternatives for healthy exercising that are creative and sensual with a professional guide.

\_\_ Take a short trip outside your usual haunts.

\_\_ Learn a new sport or improve performance you already enjoy.

\_\_ Join a club where you like the people and purpose.

\_\_ Buy some flowers or a plant.

\_\_ Have a professional massage or sauna.

\_\_ Buy or prepare some food that is healthy and savory.

\_\_ Draw, paint, or sketch something that you want to capture in your own style.

\_\_ Create a small garden inside or outside your home.

___ Buy something beautiful or stimulating for yourself and/or someone you love.

___ Start to learn or practice a creative process such as designing, acting, or painting.

Highlight the top five or so choices from this list and any of your own added preferences to choose priorities for action. If this approach works for you, create a satisfying rhythm of engaging and new activities over time. When patterns of pleasure get disrupted by the natural requirements of life, at least make a date with yourself to re-start your rewards as soon as possible. Periodically, choose completely different or spontaneous activities for variety, fun, and even challenge.

# Entrusting Yourself to People and Situations: Commitment

*An ounce of commitment is worth pounds of promises.*
Comedian and actor, Mae West

## What is commitment?

The issue of commitment, whether in relationships, work, or other matters, is a theme these days. Sometimes digging into its meaning can be useful to support action. Then its bonds with authenticity also emerge.

If you consider human nature from the perspective of its Latin root, it "is that which is being born."[8] The corresponding Greek work, *physis*, is based on the verb "to grow out of, to appear by itself.[9] According to these meanings, to be a human being is to expand your boundary, to disclose or extend yourself, rather than stand still. You reach into and out of yourself to express who you are.

The early Greeks considered such extending the self as the "willingness to act and speak at all, as a capacity to insert oneself into the world and begin a story of one's own. The hero left his hiding place, disclosing and exposing himself."[10] Being a human being or realizing your authenticity therefore typically means extending yourself.

Boundaries shift as you reach out, give, enlarge, and take in. In that process, your sense of self could become vulnerable. That's because with each of these possibilities, there's a potential loss of part of yourself or at least the feeling that's happening. But you still have the security founded on appreciating and expressing your core self, who you truly are. Couple this with the natural flux and growth of living to continuously renew yourself.

Since commitment is a process of entrusting yourself to another person, idea, belief, or situation, small wonder it can seem and be difficult. Yet, the smart risks you take with others can help build trust and confidence in yourself; you prove what you can handle. Add the spice of humor to lighten what can seem like a thick stew. Appropriate expectations for yourself and others help as well.

According to social psychologist Marjorie Fiske, four types of commitment are:

- **interpersonal** which refers to being involved with others

- **altruistic** which includes ethical, philosophical, or religious allegiances

- **mastery** which relates to work as well as play

- **self-preservation** manifested in a "lifelong need for continual reinforcement so deep-seated and pressing that it precludes the development of serious commitments of other kinds"[11]

Although the last point would seem to trump the other three, Fiske finds a uniting theme: seeking meaning in life. In addition to this general focus, there are overlaps among the themes. Ethical commitments can relate to considerations of mastery and interpersonal relations, for example.

The more you explore how you make commitments, or avoid them, the more complex they may seem. For example, commitment is a cognitive or intellectual process.

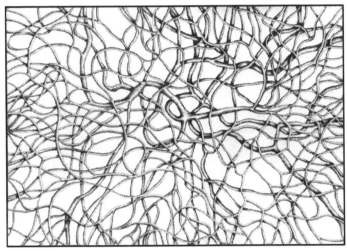

© *Drawing by Ani Bustamante*

### Some interconnections seem simple, others complex, until you follow a thread of meaning within the messiness of it all.

Reflecting purposefulness, it requires judgment. At the same time, commitment also has a non-rational or emotional aspect. Doubt is never entirely erased; discomfort, anxiety, and fear can intrude.

An especially significant commitment often involves a leap of faith in order to take action. Though impulsiveness can be an aspect, movement forward is best tempered by careful exploration of pros and cons or risks and benefits. Attention to your intuition and instincts is equally valuable.

Just as in the process of realizing your true self, what may seem like a void periodically looms. But this time it relates primarily to what's outside yourself rather than what's inside. As such, you're less likely to control what happens, though you may influence it. With the natural ambiguities of behavior and situations, attending to your core characteristics becomes even more important because it provides a foundation for confidence and action.

As the process of commitment unfolds, complications often abound. There may be a tension between honoring yourself, others' concerns, and additional matters.

Yet seeking a course of action that's best can keep you stuck in the illusion that you can be entirely objective, according to philosopher David Norton. Supporting this view is continuing research on unconscious bias or the tendency everyone carries that affects how they perceive or interact with others.[12]

As a result, you may get trapped in believing you can stand outside yourself, fully understanding what is going on or who another person is, or what a situation holds. Instead, focus on choosing what you truly want to do. Then you'll be expressing the self you are as well as striving to become. In turn, what you do is more likely to contribute to your own situation and to others.[13]

Yet making your choice about what you will do is just the beginning of commitment, as you likely have found out already. The hard part is sustaining it through all the twists and turns of your and others' preferences and actions as well as situational shifts.

This complex challenge is easier said than done. Patience and persistence must reside with being open to negotiation and external shifts. Keep invoking your sense of humor for balance. Make time to rest your body, spirit, and mind in order to use your powers well. Refer to and use the list of pleasurable activities a few pages back. Actually schedule regular time out. How many hours a week are possible? When will you start?

© *Photograph by Amé Solomon*

### *Gnomes are supposed to guard treasures. What will you do to nurture your own body?*

Trying to escape the natural ambiguity in commitments can sometimes make you want to flee to some kind of haven or hideout. Another avoidance pattern is putting one foot in your commitment and the other poised to leave. You may have seen this behavior in the approach-avoidance dance of some romantic partners.

Still another distraction from honoring commitments can be over-doing something to gain acceptance and perceived success. Priorities then disappear along with your authentic self because prime time and energy are focused primarily on one matter. Or putting other's needs usually ahead of your own, however seemingly selfless, can have similar outcomes.

Motivations for such tendencies may relate to:

- comfort with predictable habit

- sense of guilt

- preference for dependency

- avoidance of disapproval from saying "no"

- misplaced ambition

Such unproductive dances away from the complexity of commitment can sabotage the meaning and potential of an initial choice. Though overdoing or under doing something may seem a way to avoid pain or failure, each tends to work against your own empowerment and progress.

Here is a metaphor that portrays how these dynamics of commitment avoidance could work: Imagine creating a marvelous meal, but overcooking or undercooking it. The flavor and enjoyment are lost. Ingredients are either indiscernible or raw. Inattention to the appropriate process ultimately leads to an unsatisfying outcome; participants may become uninterested, uncomfortable, or even sick. The original interest in the effort and situation dissipates or gets lost.

## Being wholehearted, or not...

If "only a wholehearted choice is a choice,"[14] how do you know when to negotiate or redefine a commitment? Here is a selection of indicators for figuring out when to address problems or blocks related to your choices:

- *Body hints:* Negative stress from an unhealthy commitment may show up with regular insomnia, intestinal and skin problems, headaches, or lack of energy.

- *Repetitive issues*: Similar interpersonal problems keep repeating themselves.

- *Avoidance*: Hesitation to address issues postpones better outcomes or at least clarity about what to do that's in your interests.

- *Emotional blocks*: Fear or anxiety about imagined repercussions and vulnerabilities stymies action.

- *Missing vitality*: Joy, happiness, engagement, ease, and/or humor are not experienced or infrequent.

In addition to being alert for such hints to re-visit your commitment, use these resources and approaches to check out, improve your situation, or even let go of a commitment, after making time for due consideration:

- your intuition or gut feeling

- insights you've obtained from previous, related situations, or past patterns of behavior you don't want to repeat

- conversations with appropriate professionals and trusted, respected friends, colleagues, and family who know you truly well

- relevant, credible, written resources, online and in print

- journal or note-keeping over time in order to listen to yourself, hear your own wisdom as well as avoidance, and download repetitive thoughts from your mind

## Your challenge and choice

How will you know when to move from thinking to acting, without waiting until irreversible damage is done, becoming worn out, or indifferent to improving a situation? Although there is no neat formula for this, usually the symptoms, processes, and tools mentioned above will at least provide alerts to when you're repeating the same patterns and behaviors over and over again.

Postponement of addressing limiting habits at least saps energies and possibilities; more importantly, it keeps you from a range of better alternatives. So be alert to when you're avoiding or making incorrect or impulsive moves. That could be a sign it's time to transcend analysis, talking, mulling, and reviewing to take wholehearted, responsible action — with or without assistance.

All in all, commitment is a process rather than an isolated act, just as realizing your courage is. And as you've no doubt experienced, it is rarely neat because your behavior, relationships, and situations are in flux as well as interactive. Nevertheless, you may influence them through your choices and actions. Other people are usually beyond your control.

As you proceed, protect, and enhance your time and energy. Do this by choosing commitments that match your values, goals, and interests, or at least situations where outcomes can reflect them as closely as possible. A test of your good judgment and intuition in managing your commitments is distinguishing when it's in your interest to be fully engaged, to negotiate, or to move on. All of that will benefit from practice and paying attention to your emotions, body, spirit, and mind —as well as sometimes seeking and using good counsel.

# Appreciating Your Passions: Emotions that Energize Commitment

*There is vitality, a life-force, an energy, a quickening that is translated through you into action and because there is only one of you in all of time, this expression is unique. And if you block it, it will never exist through any other medium and be lost.*

Dancer and choreographer, Martha Graham

## Your passion is a catalyst for action

Aside from the importance and appeal of a person, idea, or situation, what prompts your commitment? There is a range of other possibilities. They include beliefs and ethics. Perhaps there is a need for self-preservation or mastery. Maybe a vision, purpose, or goal engages you. And then there's the chemistry of significant relationships that often provides glue.

But something more powerful probably propels you to act. You feel emotions such as excitement or hope. Such passions mark what truly means something to you.[15] Then, what is the meaning of passion?

The word itself started with pain: the Latin for suffering or enduring as in the passion of Christ. In the early 1200s, the meaning evolved to a strong emotion or desire, perhaps related to controlling sexual desire in a time of constraint tested by the romantic troubadours. It took over three hundred years more for passion to lose some of its sexual and suffering connotations. Today, a passion can relate to almost any strong or extravagant enthusiasm or desire for a person, thing, activity, belief, or idea.

As your passions provoke action, so can energy for self-realization be released. Yet there can be vulnerability in what you do. Implicit in authentic action is your caring enough to commit. As you probably already know, when you care, you may get hurt.

So continue attending to the risks and benefits of caring. Expect and accept some discomfort as you follow through on what's important enough to you to do. In fact, such feelings could be indicators of the worth of your investment. I use a little discomfort as a signal something is probably worth doing.

Offset discomfort by finding the sweet spots where commitment and passion interact. They can summon and strengthen each other to support choices that have meaning to you.

© *Drawing by Ani Bustamante*

### *Imagine how these flames at the bottom could ignite cycles of emotion, intensifying your rising energy and igniting action.*

Passions have other associations. Until recently, passions, or emotions, feelings, moods, and desires, were considered the opposite of restraint, rationality, and control. According to philosopher Robert Solomon, they are used incorrectly as excuses for loss of control, being carried away, or made foolish. He challenged this myth by showing the connection between what's labeled rational and the passions. To him, passions are actually judgments that structure your world to your purpose. They are:

> *"the very core of our existence, the system of meanings and values within which our lives either develop and grow or starve and stagnate. The passions are the very soul of our existence; its not they who require the controls and rationalizations of reason. Rather it is reason that requires the anchorage and earthly wisdom of the passions."*[16]

You might conclude that Solomon's view is just the perspective of one modern philosopher. But wait! His approach evolved from a historic line of philosophers such as David Hume who said that only passion moves us, reason has no such power.[17] Solomon says:

> *passions have the power to "convert mere things into goals and instruments....mere possibilities into ambitions, wishes, and hopes...Every value, everything meaningful, as well as everything vile, offensive and painful, comes into life through the passions.*[18]

Complementing this view are recent studies of how the brain works. Neuroscientist Antonio Damasio's exploration of the dynamics between feelings (or passions) and reason show that "The brain systems required by the former are enmeshed in those needed for the latter..." In fact, these systems are interwoven with the ones that regulate the body.[19]

The energy of your passions therefore provides power, the ability or capacity to act or perform effectively.[20] So imagine how passion and power will provide vigor for action. Damasio shows how "a connecting trail, in anatomical and functional terms, from reason to feelings to body" may result.[21] Then the process of giving yourself to someone or something is likely to have so much more potency, depth, and excitement.

## What are your passions?

To clarify your own passions, be alert to patterns in answers to some of the questions below that you think will provide useful information and insight. After this list is some guidance for organizing and interpreting what you notice.

- I always feel exhilarated after:

- I never tire of:

- I always want to learn about:

- The cause closest to my heart is:

- I feel masterful when:

- I have the greatest happiness when:

- I know I'm valuable when:

- The activities that reflect my purpose in life are:

- I feel joy (not just enjoyment) when I _____

Here are some questions that will help you see themes in your responses to any of the bullets above you choose. Explore those you wish, using them and others that come to mind in order to improve your life.

- What patterns or common themes do you see in your responses?

- Which relate to relationships, play, work, or combinations?

- What passions are reflected in how you use your waking time now?

- How can you express and enjoy your passions by integrating them in your work, play, and relationships within the next several months?

- What are you assuming or avoiding that is robbing the power of your passions?

© *Photograph by Kay Brinkmann*

***One example of a passion could be connecting warmly with someone you care about.***

## Let your passions play

To start, do one modest, manageable thing you're passionate about in the next few days. What will that be? Then name a few small, related steps you can take regularly to grow and sustain that choice. Can you schedule in each week just one action to create a rhythm of your commitment to your passion that works for you?

Such continuing choices will contribute to the process of realizing your true self. They will support authentic action and clarify commitments that have meaning to you. In turn, commitment and the power of your passions can lead to deeper forms of expression and purpose in work, however you define it. You'll be more likely to feel the pleasure that comes when play and work seem inseparable — or at least overlapping.

# Expressing Yourself through Creating What You Value: Vocation

> *All good work is self-revelation.*
> Film director, Sidney Lumet

## Bringing together passions, commitment, authenticity, and work

I hope that you've experienced some work, whether paid, volunteer, or at home, that is so engaging it feels like play — at least most of the time. Then you'll have a sense of how work can bring meaning to life as well as contribute to identity and self-sufficiency.

Unfortunately, too much of the language and associations related to work today seem confining or dreary. For example, do your eyes glaze over when you consider pay scale, hours of work, ladders, specializations, titles, job descriptions, niches, schedules, and complicated, shifting benefits?  However important, they hardly ignite the passions.

These days, work requirements seem to be increasing and encroaching on personal time. Electronic tethers, such as laptop computers, the range of tablets, and smart phones have created a norm of constant connection. This technology often results in many employees and self-employed people at all levels doing more than before, at all hours. Will these new norms and rhythms ultimately lead to satisfaction or even greater productivity?

## *Who's in charge? The technology or you?*

Since 2004, the end of the first Web era, annual productivity growth has dropped from 3 to 1.5 %. Though the answers about the impact of the iPhone, for example, are inconclusive, Northwestern University economist Robert J. Gordon thinks it's done "absolutely nothing" to improve productivity.

At other levels, what is the effect of career ladders, specialization, and silos on exploration, creativity, and innovation? Hiring is often dictated by the fit between current content knowledge, past experience, and what's needed immediately rather than appreciation of transferable skills and potential.

As a result, natural learning curves which eventually peter out into boredom and burnout are neither anticipated nor acknowledged early enough. Instead, specialization and current credibility can become traps due to employer inflexibility and employee comfort with labels. Such narrow definitions of what people want to and can do then keep individual development and ultimately human contribution to significant aspects of economic growth in check.

Though you personally probably cannot change such employment processes and preferences, you may have some choices about what, how, when, why, and where you work. One way to explore the value of any kind of work to you is to imagine your associations with not working, whether by choice or otherwise. For example, think about how that would affect any one or two of the following connections or associations you'd want to explore.

- identity

- pleasure in life

- security or survival

- dignity

- self-respect

- freedom

- expertise

- interests and passions

- relationships

- activities

- purpose or meaning

- time

Add other considerations to this list that come to mind that are more important to you. But for now, these twelve matters related to the quality of work, paid and unpaid, and life are probably more than enough to choose from.

The nature of your reactions to any that have particular meaning for you could tell you whether or not current work is a positive, neutral, or limiting force in your life. You'll also get inklings of your underlying assumptions about the significance to you of work in general and how you may enhance current and future efforts.

## What is your current situation?

Perhaps you imagine or find that being "workless" expands your freedom, pleasure in life, and identity. Or issues of security and survival are so crucial that everything pales in comparison. You work to live.

Use insights about limiting aspects of work to explore how you can improve your situation. The positive connections will help you decide where you want to invest further. The neutral aspects show possible areas to explore for enrichment.

After all, work often takes most of the time you're awake. Assuming at least a forty-hour work week and about eight hours of sleep per day, you have left 72 hours of supposedly discretionary time. That's with a fairly uncomplicated life in which extended work hours, chores, family matters, social life, and health issues take much of that remaining time.

Whatever your degree of weekly wiggle room, those 40+ hours of work still provide opportunities to improve your quality of life. Examples include learning, developing, and deepening relationships of value as well as improving security. As you may imagine, focus on meaning and satisfaction can bloom when you define work beyond just a source of making money, assuming you have or can create that luxury. One way to do this is to address this question: "How can I earn the living I want and do work that has meaning to me?"

## Labels to clarify what earning your living means to you

Ways to label earning your living include: job, work, career, and vocation. How you label what you do can lead to a self-fulfilling prophecy.

Matthew Fox explores the word "job" in *The Reinvention of Work*. Discussing the relationship between work and job, he mentions the Middle English "gobbe," from which "job" derived. It meant "lump." In his famous eighteenth-century dictionary, Dr. Johnson defined job as "petty, piddly work; a piece of chance work."

According to the American Heritage dictionary, work is toil or labor, neither particularly uplifting. A more positive definition is "physical or mental effort or activity directed toward the production or accomplishment of something."

Career sounds more engaging. It's a "chosen pursuit; a profession or occupation and the general course or progression of one's life." Careers are generally available to people with higher education or advanced training; many have much going for them because of their experience and accomplishments, regardless of formal credentials.

Yet even this way of looking at work is often confined to ladders and paths, slots and positions, with actual and implied boundaries set by others. Does a mere job title or one of those dry job descriptions used to describe a career capture reality — what you can and want to do?

Although doing a series of activities, rather than a formal job, work, or career, might offer greater freedom of choice, such an approach could lack depth and meaning. More inspiring, to me at least, is the idea of vocation, originally based on the sense of calling in religious endeavors. This vision of what work could be allows you to define most freely the nature of what you do. It also helps avoid assuming you must squeeze into existing frameworks of a job, work, or even career, unless you want or need to, of course.

Think of vocation as an organizing idea or transcendent enterprise that gives meaning and purpose to your efforts and life. As your calling, it enables you to express who you are to yourself and others through the creation of something with tangible or intangible value. Could that be creating a product, service, art, or family — or some mixture? Does it relate to making an idea, dream, or belief come to life? There are a range of jobs and careers, including self-employment, that can emerge from this larger vision of vocation.

Depending on vision or outcomes sought, teachers can also be healers, ministers, leaders, and politicians and vice versa. Technicians can organize work into projects, ensure effective use of resources, and train others. Receptionists can set the tone for an entire organization as well as improve communication, internally and externally. Doctors can do research, solve problems, educate, heal, collaborate, advocate, improve medical processes, and develop information systems. A soldier can build teams, teach, lead, and protect. A mother or father can be a leader, manager, and community organizer. Any of these possibilities also offer opportunities for integration of more than one aspect.

I see my vocation as providing inspiration, guidance, and tools to help people realize their true capacities. For me, that involves writing, speaking, consulting, and community building, among other ways to reach out. Though few people may see the links among my previous work as a professor, diplomat, and management consultant, that theme was also present.

While you could have one to over 10 jobs in a lifetime, imagine how much more meaningful and flexible, perhaps even secure and lucrative, work might be if it reflected your vision of a vocation. By defining and committing to the outcomes you want to foster rather than identifying with just a title, links among what you do could become more obvious and powerful.

Bottom line? Even if your time on earth is not elastic, your vocation and other ways you earn your living can be.

As with many valuable ways of seeing possibilities, this idea of vocation as an organizing vision for work is not new. Over a century ago, Max Weber envisioned what vocation would mean to an individual. In his essay on Politics and Vocation, he wrote:

> *...it is immensely moving when a mature man — no matter whether old or young in years — is aware of a responsibility for the consequences of his conduct and really feels such responsibility with heart and soul. He then acts by following an ethic of responsibility and somewhere he reaches the point where he says, 'Here I stand; I can do no other.'*[22]

Such commitment is more powerful when it's dynamic, especially as it blends the expression of passion and authenticity. By developing and periodically renewing your sense of vocation or purpose you're more likely to experience an integrated, satisfying life — as well as realize your capacity for courage.

These interactive processes also empower and enrich your professional and personal relationships. Ends and means can be in sync. You could then escape from the limits imposed by your role, what you do by others' lights, and where you fit in. Rather, who you are, what you offer, what you want, and how you will make contributions are foundations of vocation-building.

Now, you may rightly ask, "What about the practical parts of life?" Attending to the romantic-sounding idea of vocation may seem in conflict with how to:

- earn money and benefits that suit your desired level of living

- create security for the present and future

- do something others value

- have power and influence

- fulfill norms and perceived expectations of society, social group, and family

For many people, these important, practical considerations overtake asking questions about the meaning and true value of their efforts. Maybe that's one of the reasons why less attention is paid to vocation than to doing and keeping work or getting a job. These practical aspects of living are more familiar and could be easier to address, especially in the short run. But can they alone lead to a life you truly want?

Yet there are many ways to combine the visionary and practical. Perhaps start with being curious, using your imagination and clarifying what's truly important to you. Some examples: a mother or father could create a successful home-based business that promotes community. A CEO could steer her business to socially responsible activities. In fact, social entrepreneurship is an increasingly appealing option for many. What would engage or inspire you? How would you define the purpose of your life now?

## Exploring ways to define how your vocation may be expressed

Anyone can have a vocation. Neither years of education nor credentials are always necessary. Age is generally irrelevant. You don't have to belong to a group, organization, or institution or have an impressive, or even understandable, label. "All" you need is willingness to explore your vision or purpose.

Be open to trial and error as you investigate what has meaning to you or refine what you already know. Engage in conversation with good listeners who share interests. Stay open to modification while attending to authenticity, commitment, and passion.

89

Identify and synthesize related expertise and experience you have or can develop to support your progress.

Your focus for vocation can evolve over time, emerge quickly, or go through iterations. Sometimes looking back for themes in your life will help. Don't expect implementation to be neat, though. The process can include repetition, periods of stasis, and cycles.

Occasionally, progress occurs with a great leap forward. But assessing how that happened could show the leap was not as magical as it seems. Many modest steps as well as seeming detours, not to mention luck, usually contributed. Recognizing those realities can help provide patience to continue.

Take, for example, the baseball Hall of Famer who spent the first 15 years of retirement playing golf and traveling. Eventually he became bored. During some honest introspection, he realized he'd been a sourpuss on the field, expressing little real pleasure about his work.

At mid-life, he asked himself what *would* have meaning to do — a step toward determining his next vocation, if he considered playing baseball his first one. That inquiry led to a new focus at 53.

© *Drawing by Ani Bustamante*

## *Reach out from your core or center to explore a range of possibilities.*

He decided to coach the lowest ranking minor league team in his area because he wanted to help people, perhaps the first time he tied his work to others' needs. He started slowly with just a one-year contract.

"Easy for him," you may say. He had security, fame, and choice. Well, whatever your situation, first focus on exploring what might be a vocation for yourself and then be concerned about how to earn your living and other important, practical matters. Trying to wrap the package before giving the gift of choice to yourself probably won't work.

In fact, creating an air-tight plan to accomplish anything of value at the outset could sabotage the journey to vocation. It's often the small steps that help you define and test your vision. Expect slogs and loops as well as leaps forward, as with many valuable experiences. Inspiration will help, as will other people, but epiphanies and quick transformations are not typical.

For another perspective, re-visit your own experience as a child or parent. Or talk to mothers and fathers raising relatively healthy, sane, responsible children (an accomplishment in itself!).

What created and sustained their authenticity, commitment, and passion? Many had little idea of what was really involved at the outset. Yet they persisted in the vocation they chose. They learned and struggled as well as found joy and pleasure in the child's and their own progress, however messy and challenging the process. No doubt inspired stubbornness coupled with genetic predispositions and assistance from others helped.

Another example is the veterinarian who saved the eyesight of the successful racehorse Smarty Jones who almost lost his eye in a starting gate accident. If it weren't for her decision to go against conventional wisdom to remove the eye, Smarty most likely would have been put out to stud earlier. Instead, her passion for animals led her to change his bandage at 20-minute intervals for three days. I think that depth of commitment shows love of her work as well as her charges. Passion, commitment, and, no doubt, authenticity combined as she demonstrated her vocation.

Being a veterinarian is not a pre-requisite if you have a passion for animals, though. As with many conventional titles, exploring related alternatives can open a range of possibilities. Consider for example, being an animal or owner trainer, Animal Planet television personality, photographer, or community educator and activist about care. Or design your own vision by integrating what is important to you about animals.

Some seem lucky, talented, and inspired enough to latch onto a vocation fairly early, though this can lead to a yearning for refreshment, a need to find new versions later. The story goes that King of Swing Benny Goodman first picked up a clarinet at around four years of age. Over the years, though, Goodman had ups and downs and needed to shift himself periodically. Besides, most people are not so endowed. Nor are they easily able to make a go of their art by combining it with business, in his case creating and leading a group that became a popular orchestra.

Your vocation may be less public or dramatic, initially less obvious to others or even to yourself. Or an early choice may need to be renewed, reframed, or changed. Lawyers could become advocates, lobbyists, professors, writers, policymakers, or politicians; waitresses, creators of community and entertainers, and farmers, ecologists, educators, and entrepreneurs.

An example of actual struggles within a vocation is architect Bernard Tschumi's description of the worst thing about his work which sounds just like vocation when the whole is considered: "You go through great efforts in the middle of the project for the joy of the beginning when you come up with the ideas and the end when you see it built."[23] His vision emerges through the necessary slog of persistence.

However romantic vocation may sound to outsiders, it is often a demanding, complex way to earn a living and to live. Within the vignettes above, your own experience, and insights you'll have from talking to people who are deeply engaged in what they do are challenges and disappointments. Yet the super glue is provided by periodic, surprisingly positive outcomes. There can be joy in starting something fresh, of moving beyond the known and safe.

Attending to some examples such as the ones just given certainly offers both reality test and inspiration. But that does not substitute for your own exploration of what *you* want to do.

## Your vocation

If you haven't yet developed a clear idea about your vocation, either looking forward or backward, use any questions below to start. Your responses and the insights you get will help you express your calling or at least give it better focus. For now, play with, write about, and discuss any that appeal to see what emerges.

- What subjects, issues, and problems always grab your attention, interest, and emotions?

- What kinds of groups and organizations seem to be chasing visions or have ambitions that would engage you?

- What subjects and activities engaged you in high school or even before and why (if you remember!)?

- What activities do you always choose when you can? Is the common theme empowering others, unraveling a mystery, telling a story, building something tangible or intangible, or leading a team, for example? How would such processes translate to, or be integrated in the content of what you want to do? Think about the metaphors as well as the facts and information that emerge.

- Who are your role models or people whose lives intrigue you? What do they do and how do they live? Specifically, how did they become who they are? (Perhaps read their biographies or listen to them being interviewed.) What could be your own version?

- What combinations of skills, abilities, knowledge, or perspectives do you have that seem unique or original in themselves? No matter if what you offer is difficult to describe in conventional terms. Instead, state briefly how you could bring your capacities together in meaningful, inspiring ways for yourself and possibly to benefit others.

## Suggested first steps

Perhaps start by first synthesizing into common themes and then stringing together the key phrases related to:

- subjects and issues that engage
- specific transferable skills you enjoy using
- kinds of people you want to serve and work with
- venues or situations you prefer to work in

If this approach does not work for you, choose or adapt one or two options from the following. Maybe this will spark action or at least provide hints for future focus

- What would you want to do even if you weren't paid? Why?

- What thoughts, actions, goals, and relationships motivate and energize you? What patterns do you see in your choices?

- What activities drain or bore you? What kinds of people tire you? (Your answers to both or either question can tell you what you need to avoid.)

- What concrete outcomes would you want to work toward?

- Learn from others when you change a conversation opener from "What do you do?" to "What are your interests?" When it's appropriate, ask: "What are your passions?" or "What inspires you?"

© *Photograph by Andrew Winter*

### *Take flight in your imagination to observe the landscape from above.*

Maybe your vocation is not so much a subject or integration of subjects, but an issue or problem to address. Perhaps it's processes such as community-building through the arts in particular situations or leading and inspiring certain kinds of people to do their best. Or maybe creating inventions, designing products, or providing services that contribute to quality of life is your theme. Or could it be marketing products or ideas that have meaning to you?

By all means, pose your own questions as well to help clarify your vocation. Your answers to any you choose among the suggestions above and whatever else comes to mind will contain recurring themes. Use them to help you appreciate the natural complexity of your interests and passions as well as to focus and identify priorities. As you begin to express your ideas for vocation, whether new or refreshed, stay open to refinements through conversations, study, and other explorations over time.

But if what you learn doesn't uncover some hints to explore or pursue, stay alert while giving yourself a date to return to the investigation. You just may not be ready or the timing is not yet right.

Meanwhile:

- Collect leads from what you are doing and what attracts you now.

- Experiment with volunteer work that honors your strengths or stretches you as well as other low-risk opportunities. Use these experiences to test some of your inclinations and to meet people more closely involved in activities that appeal.

- Have fun observing and participating in different situations and learning about areas and fields that intrigue you.

- Explore a variety of the arts, from hip hop to crafts to Gregorian chant, that bring pleasure, culling ideas, themes, and leads as you go.

- Leave regular time to do nothing to see what percolates up from gently simmering hints within.

Given the long life most people will have into their late 60s, 70s, 80s, and even 90s, the more engaged you can be in what has meaning for you, the healthier you're likely to continue to be. The more security and enjoyment you'll have too! And during younger years, even when conventionally successful, you'll benefit from exploring beyond the obvious and predictable. "Oh, the places you'll go," as Dr. Seuss' last book and his fellow Dartmouth students said.

If you haven't already seen some fresh possibilities, it's never too late to get closer to your vocation through your job, work, career, and other activities, paid or not. When the clues within aren't already there, keep reaching out for new experiences and connections in more fertile fields to see what emerges.

You'll know you're getting closer when you:

- feel sustained energy and excitement

- love to think about what you do or will do

- believe that what has meaning to you can also go beyond meeting your own needs.

Other indicators will come when you won't be able to distinguish between work and play, can't wait to start on related matters, and time flies. Your vocation will continue to renew most of the time rather than fatigue or bore you. Not bad recipes for a good life — especially as you update your views and skills with experience and study. Then you'll be in continuous explorer mode, refreshing what engages you and yourself.

The good news: Given your likely long life span, variety awaits. You may not do just one thing or even a series of related things. As you reach a level of mastery through traveling your learning curve, refresh yourself. Try sabbaticals as well as developing new skills, knowledge, and abilities. Combine new experience and established expertise, even creating a vocation or work that has never existed as you operate independently, in collaboration, or find an organization that works for you.

Or you could do several things at once as management consultant Charles Handy chooses. Recognizing the obsolescence of retirement, he combines his careers and vocations into a portfolio including fee and gift work, reading and keeping current about his profession, and housework, to free his wife to pursue her vocation, photography.

Despite generational differences, chronological age becomes less important over time. With longer, healthier lives, the aging process is not an automatic downward slope. Life is less linear and neat, less "staged." Opportunities for growth and enjoyment occur at any point, as your process of becoming authentic, making commitments, expressing passions, and clarifying vocations continues.

# STEP THREE:
# Identifying Internal Barriers to Progress:Discomfort, Fear, Anxiety, Suffering, Guilt, and Imprints

## Find promise instead of pain in negative emotions and other blocks

*I have learned that nothing is quite so permanent as change.*
*It is simply part of living and should not be feared.*
Senator Robert Byrd when he stepped down as Appropriations
Chair at 90.

*I dwell in possibility...*
Poet, Emily Dickinson

*The process of becoming courageous involves the willingness to realize your true capacities by going **through** discomfort, fear, anxiety or suffering and taking wholehearted, responsible action.*
Definition of the process of becoming courageous
from Ruth Schimel's dissertation research

This Step will help you start to free yourself to express your capacity for courage. As you read and take small steps, you'll find ways and means to go *through* strong negative emotions and transcend confining psychological imprints. The incremental guidance is designed so you can tailor it to your needs. Graphics are included to engage you further in the experience. All together, you'll find tools, explanations, and inspiration to support the choices you make.

Though you can dip into the Six Steps of *Choose Courage* at any point to make progress, at least explore this aspect of the process to loosen the shackles of negative influences. Your investment can keep you from staying stuck now and getting distracted in the future.

Now to encourage yourself — Believe it or not, experiencing discomfort, fear, anxiety, suffering, or guilt can be a surprising, if perverse, gift. In other words, what causes pain may be a source for healing when addressed.

*The Emotional Life of Your Brain* by Richard Davidson and Sharon Begley, as well as neuroscientist Antonio Damasio's work, provide additional hope for what is called neuroplasticity. That's the ability of the brain to add and rework capacity and connections, and to develop compensatory mental processes with practice. Additional good news is that this can happen regardless of age and limitations.

Davidson, Begley, and Damasio, along with other researchers and authors, explain how thought and emotion are connected biologically. Though often seen as opposites in Western culture, rationality and feeling are necessary for full use of capacities. They complement and strengthen development and growth. Facing and transcending negative emotions and influences will then allow space for positive ones to emerge, releasing energy for continuing action. These dynamic opportunities show up in the very word: e-motion.

Expressions of negative emotions could range from the distraction of unease to an overwhelming sense of great pain. Effects vary from distortion of good judgment to loss of control to missed opportunities. (Please keep in mind that Step Three and

Step Four are not designed for anyone with severe mental illness and/or chemical imbalances.)

© *Photograph by Andrew Winter*

***A flower as metaphor: This unique flower is organized as a hub with connections to other parts of itself. Similarly, your thoughts and emotions can send out energy that are spokes of growth from your essential core self.***

In nature, as well as human behavior, there are many metaphors and images that capture the complex processes of how the body and brain, or mind if you wish, interact and support one another. They can help you imagine the opportunities in what often seems like paradox, or contradiction. They also provide a doorway to actual and abstract beauty itself, to awe about the stunning complexity and richness of our bodies, particularly the brain. In turn, such understanding and associations can support integration of thought and emotion versus mere impulsive reaction.

As far back as the 1600s, Sir Frances Bacon said, "Nothing is to be feared but fear itself."[24] Maybe some ancient Greek said it earlier. We know President Franklin Delano Roosevelt did in relation to

World War II. It's still apt, I think. If you wish, keep this suggestion in mind as you practice facing whatever fear you have of negative emotions.

No matter who said what or the opportunities in negative emotions, who wants emotional pain or even discomfort? Yet they often accompany the very nature of living fully. Along the way, you're likely to encounter disappointments, losses, pressures, threats, conflicts, and problems, among other challenging experiences. Naturally, your responses will vary. But your power lies in the choices you make to deal with them.

To explore those choices, place a check on the line to the left of all examples below that reflect your current productive tendencies for dealing with negative emotions. For example, do you:

_____Name specifically and perhaps jot down for catharsis and clarity, negative emotions that disturb you?

_____Note physical symptoms as possible clues to underlying emotional issues?

_____Consider briefly, without succumbing to over thinking or repetition, what you feel, including some sources?

_____Do you use your insights to:

_____avoid or limit the radioactive fallout of private or public emotional outbursts?

_____move beyond emotional constipation or staying stuck in one feeling?

_____let go of issues you can't influence or will get you nowhere?

_____find ways to use your energy and time to support positive outcomes?

_____Translate understanding of your negative emotions to clarify top priorities and identify some useful strategies?

____Assess how your time, main values, and accessible resources can support specific actions to transcend limiting emotions?

____Obtain assistance from informal as well as professional sources?

____Give back and "pay forward" the assistance you've received to benefit others?

____Use insights and experience to lessen the impact of limiting emotions in the future?

Or do you tend to distract yourself from taking effective action and misplace precious time and energy with any of the following responses?

____Dramatize discomfort, fear, anxiety, suffering, or guilt in your own mind or in discussions beyond what would be useful catharsis.

____Continue to focus on negative emotions rather than on what you can and will do next.

Escape into:

____overwork

____busyness and chores galore

____compulsive or excessive eating, drinking, or exercise

____focus on others' needs primarily

____worst case scenario imaginings

____attention to others' behavior instead of your own

____obsessive, repetitive thoughts

____sleep

____unhealthy relationships and situations

_____self-absorption

_____blame of others

_____Let negative emotions overwhelm you, sap your energy, or stay stuck.

_____Avoid getting assistance from appropriate personal and professional sources.

If avoidance or wallowing postpone eventually going *through* negative emotions, you'll likely limit progress toward what you want, perhaps even stay stuck or regress. But if you generally deal with such feelings in whatever incremental, productive ways work for you, then accessing your courage will become easier and more direct. Why?

First, I bet you'll just feel better in your own skin. You'll likely make improved choices, use resources more effectively, and have increased energy for action in your interest. Confidence and hope will also strengthen over time, despite the natural ups, downs, and loops of life.

As possible, modest, or even baby, steps will be more powerful when they reflect your authenticity, commitment, passion, or work that has meaning, discussed in depth in Step Two. Attending to and integrating these four catalysts for expressing your courage, will help meet goals you truly want.

For example, being straightforward about or at least exploring what you want, creates a path through the weeds of maybe this, maybe that. Such back and forth ping pong, keeps you and others from seeing what's important. It also provides excuses to avoid the very experiences and actions that could help you find out what is important as well as improve your flexibility and resilience.

Furthermore, why should others help you when you have not made the effort to clarify and present your interests clearly? And even if they'd want to assist you, regardless of your clarity, results will likely suit you better when you make your needs and preferences as apparent as possible.

As suggested in the first set of choices at the start of this Step, there are a variety of ways to wrestle effectively with emotions that distract you and fog your future. In fact, you probably have useful experience to guide you already, including aspects of the summary of those suggestions in Table 3.1 on the next page. Then, whatever your tendency, you know that making progress is easier to describe than to do.

Yet certainly, building resilience and strength by working slowly through negative emotions and related concerns is a better alternative to:

- remaining distant from what's important or enjoyable

- keeping yourself in a bland or anesthetized state that neutralizes feelings

- losing irretrievable time by postponing an action you can take to improve your situation

- revisiting regrets without learning from them and moving on

- repeating limiting or destructive behavior and possibly sinking into despair and inaction

To work through such blocks to progress and a better life, use, adapt, and add to the ideas that follow.

*Table 3.1*

## POSITIVE WAYS TO DEAL WITH NEGATIVE EMOTIONS

- Name what you feel.
- Develop some insights about sources and meaning of your emotions.
- Identify priorities and strategies for action.
- Assess and use resources, time, and values for prompting action.
- Obtain assistance.
- Start with one manageable step.
- Commit to rhythms of action that make sense.
- Use what you've learned, applying it to similar situations in the future.

# Name your emotions

Many people sense and express particular emotions differently. Influences include life experiences, genetic predispositions, and established neural pathways in your brain that result in automatic behavior, especially under stress. What is your discomfort or disquiet is another person's deep anxiety. The associations, people, and situations that charge your emotions can also be unique. (Please keep in mind that severe mental illness generally requires continuing, often interdisciplinary, professional attention.)

As already mentioned, expressing clearly what you are feeling is a first step in choosing how to address it. Yet such words may not typically be on the tip of your tongue, especially since using the language of emotion is not always comfortable, encouraged, or even acceptable.

If interested, the following offers some options for using accurate vocabulary that may help you address negative emotions. Then you'll also be in a better position to express what you are feeling to others, when you wish. In turn, they'll better understand you and you'll have clearer opportunities for action as you truly hear yourself.

© *Photograph by DigitalFreePhotos.net*

### *Manage your fiery gremlins safely, with dexterity, even if your clothes get a little stained from flipping. (You can always change or wash them!)*

Over time, self-understanding, mutual appreciation, and trust can increase. More important, though, is connecting directly with your own internal gremlins, managing the flames they ignite in the frying pan of life.

To start to move through fear and anxiety, first consider what differentiates them. The following connections and distinctions may help you parse out what you're feeling, now and later.

Existential psychologist Rollo May made an important distinction between fear and anxiety. He said the reaction "to threats to existence... and to ...values, is in its general form, anxiety."[25] Fear relates to specific dangers. So anxiety can precede and mask fear. More complex to untangle, anxiety may be the greater challenge.

How then can you determine, understand, and move beyond your sources of anxiety? More naming via theologian Paul Tillich's three types may be useful:[26]

- Anxiety about fate and death: An example could be when a sense of vulnerability or mortality is felt, either related to your own situation or someone close to you.

- Anxiety about meaninglessness or emptiness: Examples could be weakening or loss of identity, questioning the value of what you do or who you are as you rush frenetically from one activity, goal, or person to another.

- Anxiety from guilt: An example could be something significant you have or have not done related to yourself or others.

By all means, label your own types of anxiety, especially if these examples are not satisfying or relevant. Notice if they come from one source or combinations. Consider external situations such as a weak economy, behavior of someone close, bullying, dismissal by people over whom you have little influence, or a difficulty at work. Often, more uncertainty than usual in life sparks anxiety, whatever the source.

Nevertheless, according to some psychologists and probably sports coaches, a moderate amount of anxiety can also be catalytic in improving performance.[27] Knowing how much is optimal is the challenge and opportunity.

Whether from fear or anxiety, you could feel exposed or vulnerable to harm or risk. Or maybe you're connected with a particular situation in which you have little choice. Perhaps you're dealing with unpredictable, unsupportive, or dangerous people who may show threatening emotions such as on the face below.

© *Photograph by Andrew Winter*

***How could you convert a possibly threatening countenance such as this? Imagine a smile rather than a frowning, angry, shouting face on the person and proceed accordingly. Or move away.***

Since you can't count on what will happen, any large or small challenge may accentuate a negative emotion. You know where you are now, but not what's in the void between the present and what's coming. Those anxiety-producing unknowns can make you feel out of control, even lost. This occurs especially when you continue to postpone dealing with a crucial issue or a series of smaller, related matters over which you can exercise some influence — or for which you can muster assistance.

At such times, naming specifically what you are feeling can constrain distracting, intrusive gremlins or at least keep them bound in your own frying pan. Then exploring choices and possible consequences may contribute to some semblance of security. Once these boundaries are clear, you'll be able to do some specific, useful planning and preparation. In turn, your efforts to influence a situation can contribute to your confidence or at least some relative calm.

The following suggestions for describing emotions may help if you feel at a loss for exact words or want to explore a wider vocabulary. Possibly use these examples of definitions and associations, or add your own, for feeling fearful: terror, dread, horror, deep distress, fright, panic, scared, or alarm. Ways to describe anxiety might include: nervous, worried, distracted, disquieted, sleepless, uncertain, or uneasy.

Another key to your emotions may be as clear as the nose on your face: an actual physical expression. The graphic below could encourage you to notice such nonverbal communication — yours and others'. Since communication experts hold that the majority of communication is nonverbal, attention to such manifestations is a good investment of several seconds of your time.

To have some fun with this approach as well as to elicit insights, go beyond the examples below using the two blank faces. Draw in a few of your own expressions you see in the mirror or imagine. The experience may also deepen your understanding of how some even transitory muscular shifts in your face can say so much, whether intended or not.

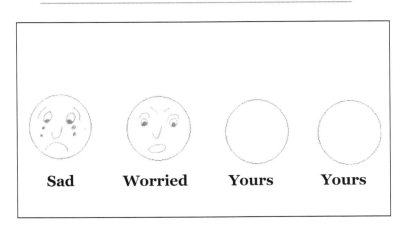

Other ways to improve understanding and descriptions of what you're feeling are:

- Have a conversation with someone you trust and respect about what's going on within you, jotting down some notes on what emerges for clarity and recall.

- Write about your concerns in a few pages or less to see what the free flow of words tells you.

- Consider one or two worst case outcomes and how you would deal with them.

- Imagine some possible positive outcomes from what seems dangerous or threatening.

- Search the Internet by typing in "synonyms for _____" to find additional definitions of emotions to explore or use a thesaurus.

- Attend to physical symptoms such as sleeplessness, nervous gestures, or heart palpitations as cues and clues to fear and more likely anxiety.

- See what emotions any of the arts or sports that attract you evoke; then name what bubbles up from within.

# Accept emotions

As they say in twelve-step programs, after you name your emotions, claim them. In other words, admit what you are feeling. For example, you could say to yourself:

- When I toss and turn instead of sleeping, I sense I am feeling anxious about _____.

- When I bury myself in work or other activities, I wonder if I'm trying to avoid my fear of_____.

- When I overeat, drink alcohol excessively, or do anything else destructive to my health, I recognize these temporary escapes are masking discomfort about_____.

- When I push myself or someone else beyond what makes sense, what am I overcompensating for, avoiding, projecting, inappropriately controlling, or trying to prove?

- When I use every opportunity to avoid a situation or individual, what is the underlying issue?

To start to transcend such matters, use your intuition and imagination to explore what's behind negative themes that keep repeating in your mind. What specifically could there be in a past experience or situation that presses your buttons? Perhaps consult with people who know you well or a professional.

Based on these insights identify one or two manageable, practical actions that may help release you from the hold of negative thoughts and emotions. To build on what you're learning, experiment with doing one related thing within the next few days. What and when will that be?

# Dump discomfort, fear, or anxiety

Now that you have named and claimed what you are feeling, try the last part of the twelve-step program mantra. Think about how you can dump the emotions that are barriers to your progress.

Perhaps the suggestions below will help you do this. Adapt or add to any of them that appeal. Warning: magic unlikely. Merely thinking and talking will probably not suffice. Some time, commitment, and action are necessary!

*Write down what you feel specifically and briefly on one piece of paper or computer pane.* Then play with all the possibilities for destroying that written record. Possibly, crumple and throw it into irretrievable garbage. Burn or tear it into tiny pieces. Flush the pieces down the toilet. Erase it from the computer, if you're using that. Or choose another way that works for you to let go, saying goodbye to what's holding you back.

*Try a creative way to express what you are feeling for fun and to remind yourself of your abilities.* One possibility is a narrative paragraph of several lines describing accomplishments of any nature that give you pride. Others could include a very short story, poem, lyric, private dance, ditty or song, drawing, positive motto for yourself, or mantra.

*Keep a mini-journal on index cards, in a small notebook, smart phone, or computer file.* Specify what you want to let go, without dwelling a great deal on what keeps you stuck. After writing up to a few pages, stop. If possible, let a few days go by without thinking about it. (Use the Supreme's STOP gesture described within the next few pages if you do repeat the same thoughts.)

Next review what you wrote to identify main insights and patterns as well as what you don't want or can't afford to repeat.

Commit to one related action within a few days. Such writing can download from your mind recurring, draining thoughts and feelings; the action itself may move you forward.

The entire process can also unclutter your mind, leaving room for clearer, more productive thinking and positive emotions. You'll then be more likely to feel some well-founded and deserved peace as well as be ready to face the continuing challenges of everyday life.

*Experiment with using an appealing, manageable daily or weekly routine to take attention away from negative emotions.* Develop self-nurturing natural rhythms. For example, select a regular time each day or week to have a short conversation with yourself about priorities and pleasures for the time ahead. At the end of the day or week, acknowledge accomplishments, however modest.

To try this, choose among, adapt, or add to any of the following.

- Develop a few ideas for right proportion between work and other activities. Make small behavioral adjustments that lead to fun and learning about matters that challenge and engage you. They can cross-fertilize, enhancing more than one aspect of your life.

- Bring greater depth and breadth into your relationships by widening connections and strengthening intimacy.

- Engage your senses through exercise, exposure to new sights, and sensual pleasures.

  http://www.ted.com/talks/bernie_krause_the_voice_of_the_natural_world.html?utm_source=newsletter_weekly_2013-07-20&utm_campaign=newsletter_weekly&utm_medium=email&utm_content=talk_of_the_week_button

- Eat and drink in healthy ways; start with a simple description of your goals. Perhaps Google Harvard Healthy Living Plate for some current, straightforward guidance.

Processes of re-balancing will probably take some time, especially within a constantly shifting life. Just stay alert to establishing and refining patterns and processes that serve your interests and satisfy you. And even then you could find it challenging to sustain consistent approaches. In such cases, avoid recriminations and return to your good focus. Keep rewarding yourself for any progress.

By all means, keep experimenting to find what works for you to avoid boredom, insensitivity to routines, and meaninglessness. And if you move away significantly from plans and processes that have worked well for a while, be kind to yourself. Just start again, adjusting action to what now makes sense.

Possibly gather a few partners for mutual encouragement. To reinforce any progress, use a variety of rewards that satisfy you all. As with the process of becoming courageous, incremental, iterative actions are more likely to work and hold up.

And finally, humor and playfulness can be beneficial as well. Co-opt the Supremes' song: *Stop in the Name of Love* (of yourself!). If you can't visualize their body language of a traffic cop with palm raised out in front motioning "*stop*," imagine what you would do to emphasize the word.

Maybe come up with your own song, a dance, movement, or some nonverbal equivalent for *stop* that makes you smile while delivering the message to yourself and abiding by it. Or get in the mood by listening to about 3.5 minutes of the old Supremes' video of the song: http://www.youtube.com/watch?v=iDPjYZxion8

With or without the Supremes' help, the process of letting go of negative emotions will probably not be an overnight sensation.

From experience, you already know that life is neither neatly linear nor logical. That's one of the reasons why *Choose Courage* is designed so you can dip into it at any point that seems useful to you. Processes can be circular, blunted, inconclusive, productive, and progressive; almost all provide opportunities for learning, though.

## Appreciate what the power of your body contributes

As mentioned at the beginning of this Step, many biological processes are metaphors as well as representative of life's complexity. In addition to the billions of neurons in the brain, the approximately 45 foot long gut has its own nervous system, second to the brain's most numerous neurons.

When you want to listen to your gut feeling as well, perhaps explore *Gut Feeling: The Intelligence of the Unconscious* by Gerd Gigerenzer. (What an apt first name for someone writing about the gut!). To me, it is a miracle that the seeming cacophony of interactions among the neurons, bacteria, and hormones in the body offer opportunities for healthy harmony, however you define it.

The variety of connections prompts concurrent and seemingly haphazard firings of information throughout the nervous system. In split seconds, these processes lead to awareness of emotion and thought, to movement and other actions.

Repetition of certain behaviors and feelings, useful and not, can create more direct paths for carrying information in your body. The result is possibly automatic responses. The question is whether or not reinforcing or succumbing to such automatic piloting is in your interest or not. There is recent research on the connectomes or hubs of neural connections in the brain, as represented metaphorically in the flower at the start of this Step. It provides fascinating insights about what this rich complexity implies and how it works.

Sebastian Seung holds in *Connectomes* that such wiring in the brain makes us who we are. If you want to explore further see his recent book. Also of value are neuroscientist Antonio Damasio's works, among many other science writers, and the magazine: *Scientific American MIND.*

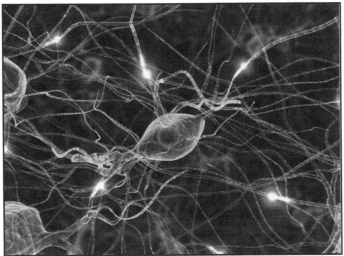

SOURCE: *news.discovery.com/tech/brain-activity-now-in-3d.html*

Even general magazines offer intriguing information such as a recent article on parasites (Toxo for short) from cats and other sources that find homes in human brains. Evidently the parasites may influence behavior, emphasizing introversion and extroversion. http://www.theatlantic.com/magazine/archive/2012/03/how-your-cat-is-making-you-crazy/8873/

Imagine how you can influence your own neural pathways with your choices and actions. Just as in a field, park, or other natural setting where people move through the land in the same way, routes can become ruts or sprout new tributaries. The paths of the neurons set down streambeds of varying depths and strengths. No wonder psychologist-philosopher William James intuitively referred to certain kinds of automatic thinking as streams of consciousness as long ago as 1892.

Through your healthy choices and actions, you'll be creating new, possibly improved, or at least less entrenched or muddy paths. They could offer a wider range of possibilities that better serve your interests.

## Continue to release your energies through self-management

To help activate your potential, embrace a seeming paradox of being patient as well as experimental. Keep remembering and honoring your important priorities and pleasures. Maybe do one thing a day you are avoiding, or at least part of it. And certainly do one small thing that's fun. Can you devote 15-30 minutes to support your progress?

As Charles Duhigg counsels in his reader's guide in the appendix to using his ideas in *The Power of Habit: Why We Do What We Do in Life and Business*:

- Identify cues and motivations that prompt the actual routine you want to change.

- Experiment with rewards that will encourage a shift in the routine.

Let your new, better habits crowd out the ones that limit you. Continue helping yourself as well as getting and exchanging assistance with others. Avoid beating yourself up or dwelling on efforts that are clearly not working; you can't force such things no matter how capable, sincere, or powerful you are. If you make a mistake or regress, ask yourself what you can learn from what happened or what you don't want to repeat.

Play with, refine, and apply ideas and suggestions from this Step in whatever order and ways that work for you. Then move on to another Step, or aspect of one, that you choose. Keep using other sources such as people, processes, and ideas you come to respect or at least find promising.

Continue to invoke your sense of humor: "There I go again! I don't need to repeat that." Always acknowledge progress, however small the step. You know the drill.

# From self-talk to action

# A math story

Unfortunately, I know how to frustrate myself as well as anyone. I've wasted too much time until I became ready to do some important things differently. One example is the trouble with math I've had since junior high school. My lack of confidence with it led me to let go of high school interests in biochemistry and architecture.

I continued to let my math gremlins haunt me even though I needed to deal with them occasionally in what I chose to do. Through decades and three degrees, statistics flummoxed me. Facing the long-postponed requirement at the doctoral level, the anxiety and even fear about the impending course kicked in again.

But even anticipating another cliffhanger grade and anxiety about struggling with the course itself didn't spur me to handle the situation better. With the requirement for graduation forcing my attention, I started with logical self-talk, my typical fallback.

Certainly, I couldn't be capable in other subjects and so inept in math. Then, what was my problem? I had already over-analyzed my relationship and issues with a discouraging teacher in junior high school and my engineer/teacher father, disappointed in me and no doubt himself because he could not help me. Yet being aware of that history didn't make a difference in my attitude, actions, and anxiety.

What I could do was stop hugging my old unproductive emotions and protective habits to my chest, stop falling back on that ineffective ego-driven approach of toughing it out by myself. What would replace this pattern?

As I admitted how ineffectual these habits were, a blinding glimpse of the obvious emerged. I could not do this by myself. I needed help.

***What peacock-like habit of pride in keeping control would you benefit from letting go?***

Voila! Then an answer appeared. Or, more likely, I became aware of the opportunity already there.

I realized a friend and colleague who was a whiz in math was having trouble with a subject I enjoyed and found accessible: organizational theory. During a conversation about our mutual woes, we agreed to tutor one another.

As she helped me learn, I remember her saying periodically, "Ruth, your eyes are glazing over." "What was that about," I asked myself. I figured out the flat look in my eyes reflected fear, my fear of being a dunce — again. The fear froze my attention, distracting me from listening and focusing on the material.

Each time that flat, blank look showed up, my friend would gently reel me back to paying attention to what we were discussing and studying. Eventually I could sense that freeze or "look" as well and pull myself back into focus on my own.

I learned to let go of the fear of failure and concentrate on the here and now, freeing myself to listen and grasp the material. With each small step, I built my base of understanding enough to strengthen confidence and hope about myself. At the end of the term, we each got A's in our courses.

The larger learning? If I ever want or need to use a quantitative approach or anything else I feel blocked about, I will find help instead of trapping myself in negative emotions and the false sense of being incapable. Unwillingness to admit to others what feels like inadequacy and misplaced pride rarely helps and usually hinders. It certainly wastes time, accentuates discomfort or suffering, and postpones creating better outcomes.

## Use dangers as cues for effective action

A difficult situation looming or something new that intimidates may be the very opportunity to take a different tack leading to growth. Instead of hiding out in the specious safety and predictability of avoidance or worry, explore how you will get assistance. Consider mutual aid, bartering, purchase of services, friendly support, and other means that make sense.

Whether on your own or as a member of group or community, challenges can also be catalysts for improved outcomes. Thoughtful collaborations can create better results, even if developing or deepening such mutually beneficial relationships seems difficult at first.

But all these suggestions are rational and people often are not. Unfortunately, the small or great crisis or recurring issue is what forces attention.

An example: Some credible experts actually anticipated the factors contributing to the deep US recession that started in 2008. Yet, few individuals and responsible institutions seemed to take notice, let alone action, until the situation became especially dire. Their embrace of the real estate bubble and its benefits, coupled with lack of incentives to act differently or even address their own collusion, kept them stuck in the dangerous status quo — until the reality of a teetering economy forced new choices. At that point, bankers, leaders, policymakers, economists, and politicians were forced to question their assumptions and other habits of thinking — called ideology by some.

Not surprisingly, power plays, vested interests, and disagreements about effective policies all fed into and distorted initial as well as later efforts. Nevertheless some crucial decisions helped avoid a worse situation.

Yet millions of people suffered and may never recoup their losses or confidence. Much smaller numbers of people did very well for themselves, and continue to do so, because they continued to understand how to play "the system" for their own benefit.

The history of such bubbles, whether real estate, dot.com, or tulips, repeats. And to this day there is still disagreement on causes, let alone "cures." A review of 21 books by an MIT professor notes the Rashomon effect with each book reflecting the particular author's perspective.

So individuals are not alone in creating their own bubbles and making dangerous choices. Why the repetition of crises and lack of attention to avoiding them? Over optimism and preference for the comfortable status quo seems to trump applying lessons from the past to dangers imbedded in the present. Receiving short-term rewards, even after failures become clearer, coupled with lack of retribution, also supports business as usual.

But the opportunity remains to appreciate the meaning of any crisis to help focus choices, whether it applies to the national economy or your own struggles. The Chinese ideograph for crisis combines danger and crucial point which is sometimes interpreted as opportunity.

See en.wikipedia.org/wiki/Chinese_word_for_%22crisis%22 for a more subtle discussion. In any event, the meaning shows why entering such scary situations is so uncomfortable for many people.

For yourself, use the feeling of danger, even a frisson of fear, as a cue to opportunity. It could be a sign of a shift to be exploited rather than ignored or shunned.

First give yourself some time to think as well as sense your emotions. Without judgment, explore what you think. Jot down the main points to keep issues from repeating in your mind and to have a record for follow up, especially for doing critical thinking with others.

Then attend to the associations and possibilities that grab your attention or excite you. Imagine a few related actions you could take. What might be likely outcomes for the most appealing one?

For any possibility that still appeals to you, have conversations about what comes to mind with people you trust and enjoy. Then make a choice for follow up within the next week. As you wish, test your approach with small, manageable steps as you explore further.

Stay alert to what your emotions and mind suggest for course corrections or next actions. Avoid automatic pilot and habits insofar as possible to ensure you bring fresh as well as effective approaches to the process. To assist with this, choose among some relevant periodicals, blogs, Web sites, articles, social networking sources, TV programs, or other resources. To benefit your thinking, make sure there's a balance between materials that challenge your approach as well as support it.

Then start moving forward. If you stay static or in student mode, the longer you postpone addressing a looming issue, the more likely it could explode, unravel, or lose value.

Even modest actions could provide inspiration for moving through whatever discomfort, fear, or anxiety you may feel. As experience brings knowledge and insight, your competence and confidence will continue to strengthen. Philosopher Paul Tillich nailed this: "Decision is a risk rooted in the courage of being free."

# Suffering

The boundaries among the four negative emotions that are part of the definition of courage can be porous. Whether in everyday or clinical experience, meanings may overlap among suffering, discomfort, anxiety, and fear. That's one reason I've clarified them all in the word-by-word definition of courage within Step Five and in the guide at its end: uncovering your courage through stories. Then, you will at least see what *I* mean!

In this definition, suffering is the feeling of actual pain or distress, sustaining loss, injury, harm or punishment; the enduring of evil, injury, pain, or death. Understandably, this experience can feel far more oppressive and physically challenging than other negative emotions.

Suffering may seem imposed, and therefore less easy to influence or control. But is this so? Where do external and internal origins start and stop? Complicating interpretation further is the unique response of each person. Such variation and ambiguity provide opportunities as well as some limitations.

As an example, people get sick. They may lose their capacity for self-sufficiency in varying degrees. Whether in months, years, or decades, eventually they die. In any situation, how individuals and loved ones learn, prepare, get assistance, respond, and sustain useful engagement with such difficulties varies depending on many factors. They can include cultural norms, genetics, willingness, and resources.

In addition to these variables, are professionals' diagnostic skills, understanding of effective treatments, and willingness to explore and collaborate with others in particular situations. Such collaboration relates to the people involved, specialists, and generalists, as well as alternative sources beyond conventional categories. Obtaining appropriate medical insurance and disability coverage in the United States can be especially hard for chronic issues, including long-term mental illness.

Another cause of suffering results from getting in harm's way, impulsively or not. There can be choices there as well. Certainly, fighting off a street robber and running after him as I did showed poor judgment. I was just lucky he did not turn and attack me. My automatic reaction probably surprised him along with myself. This could have reflected imprints from hyper alertness in the New York City subways and confidence developed from target shooting skills with a .22 caliber rifle, starting at an early age. This time, my choice was definitely not courageous by the definition in this book.

What about the individual who initially connects to an evil person or other punishing situation? Maybe that's due to any combination of naïvité, ignorance, or an unconscious imprint from past experience that supports susceptibility. The longer that connection is sustained, though, probably the harder to disengage.

At what point would that person become unable to disconnect, so dependent, conditioned, or trapped that choice is lost? Is the suffering self-imposed, beyond free choice, or somewhere in between?

A pertinent discussion of passion in Step Two relates to the pain of Christ on the cross. Centuries later the meaning of passion shifted to a feeling closer to passionate connection, whether to a person, idea, or situation. As you may imagine, suffering may even be present in such positive aspects of passion.

When explored, even this superficially, the variety of incarnations and range of interpretations of suffering seem inescapable. Consider, for example, the suffering of a woman whose love is not acknowledged, or a man whose fealty to an individual, group, or organization results in rejection, for whatever reason. When is any loving or loyal person responsible for knowing the danger and transmuting vulnerability into self-protection? Who closes or opens the door to that suffering?

Another process related to suffering involves how the 1 billion neurons in the body connect with physical experiences of pain; they vary considerably with the person experiencing it. The relationship between emotion and physical pain is likely more interactive than discrete, more complex than just simple cause and effect. Think of the phantom pain or suffering of someone with a lost limb, for example.

Speaking again of medical matters, I wonder why health care providers call us patients. No doubt a long wait to see a doctor tries one's patience, also derived from the word, to suffer.

In contrast, consider what suffering may offer. Imagine how you would respond to what author, Paulo Coelho says in the *Alchemist,* "Tell your heart that the fear of suffering is worse than the suffering itself. And that no heart has ever suffered when it goes in search of its dreams..." This association brings up the seemingly paradoxical pairing of pleasure and pain or suffering.

A quick visit to philosophy brings other ideas about what suffering could offer. Examples include:

- Hedonism was originally based on the ancient Greek Epicurus who counseled avoidance of suffering first. Pleasure lies in the ease felt after freeing oneself from the distracting pursuit of short-lived pleasures.

- Stoicism taught indifference to pleasure and pain as a way of coping.

- Utilitarianism encouraged differentiation between pleasure and pain and its measurement as a calculus for action.

Later interpreters argued that the moral status of a human being comes from the ability to feel pain and pleasure.

Given this perspective, suffering or pain can be a mark of a sentient person. Without it, meaning and perspective may be lost. Dare I say, then, that some kinds of suffering can have value? How you deal with it may provide opportunities for increased power and possibilities.

## Move beyond the self-affliction of guilt

In addition to discomfort, fear, anxiety, and suffering another internal block to action in your interest may be a feeling of guilt. That can come from avoiding fulfillment of your promise in the broad sense as well as concrete promises to yourself and others.

*Image is in the public domain believed to be free to use without restriction in the US.*

Not just a sense of remorse or unfulfilled and perhaps unreasonable expectations, guilt goes deeper. As with other negative emotions, it distracts from your own development. Guilt saps energy and self-respect, postponing the very positive e-motions that will energize you to move ahead. When you're willing and ready, you can address over time the guilt that stymies you, possibly through self-study as well as assistance from professionals and others you trust.

From Paul Tillich's point of view, moving through such guilt involves affirming yourself, or revisiting your strengths, particularly from a moral perspective. A question could be, "What have I made of myself?"[28] Another, more immediate approach is to ask: What do I want to make of myself now? When your choices reflect your values, or how you think you ought to live, moral action becomes possible.[29] Tillich believed guilt lies in the struggle between self-realization and self-denial.[30]

One path to self-realization is to develop your own personal contract of self-appreciation. Why call it a contract? That might sound business-like or cold.

First, a contract helps organize and focus thinking about your goals and resources for action. Second, since you're the one who writes it according to your vision and needs, you're more likely to honor its content and purpose as well as continue to update it. By making the contract authentic, you'll express what makes you unique, reminding yourself to act accordingly. Using your own words, versus boiler plate from other sources, will contribute to its meaning and value.

Since it's your contract, you'll probably want to avoid wasting your investment through "non-compliance." In legal terms, the contract requires some exchange, also called *consideration*.

To test its balance and likely enforceability, then, ask yourself what you are giving and what you are getting from the contract. Is it effort, work, or commitment, for example, in exchange for self-respect, success, and pleasure? What are the concrete outcomes you expect in exchange for what you provide? Are they viable?

© *Drawing by Ani Bustamante.*

### *Imagine yourself as a brave Valkyrie preparing to vanquish the dragon of guilt and self-denial.*

If you don't essentially honor your contract over time, you might miss a future you truly want. Other losses along the way could include:

- decreased confidence

- disappointment in yourself

- weakened intellectual and emotional muscles for sustaining motivation and good results

- detours or distractions from investing in what you really want to be and do

- missed opportunities

Start your contract of self-appreciation as simply as possible. Think about your current strengths. Without letting false or actual modesty depreciate you, jot down several positive qualities.

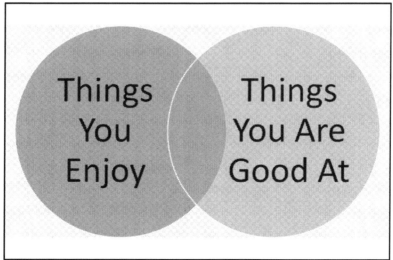

*Image is in the public domain believed to be free to use without restriction in the US.*

## In this Venn diagram, attend to what's in the overlap between your two circles.

Better to accentuate a positive perspective rather than a negative or neutral one, especially since finding the golden mean and sustaining it is unlikely anyway. In other words, some distortion or just inaccuracy occurs naturally. Then why not "err" positively in your favor?

Now keep adding to your list of strengths and other positive qualities by writing down 20+ examples. See what pops into mind as you remember those you demonstrated in handling situations and activities you enjoyed or gave you pride. Avoid second guessing yourself by thinking of how you fell short in any way.

If you wish, solicit and include positive written and oral feedback from a few people who appreciate your positive qualities. Though this is not usual in our society, the experience can lead to an improved appreciation of yourself as well as some relationships. Identify two to three people willing to take some time to think, people who know you from sharing work and other activities where they've seen you in action. Ask them to mention only specific, positive aspects about you, preferably giving examples based on their experiences with you as well as observations. Offer to do the same for them.

Keep adding to and clarifying your list over time. Refer to it periodically, possibly once a month to remind yourself of powers you want to continue expressing.

If this seems corny, sappy, or just self-indulgent, think of how many times you've received accurate, positive feedback about yourself or even provided it for others. What is lost by filling such a likely void? And what is gained?

If you have trouble getting started or expanding your list, maybe you're just not used to acknowledging your specific strengths. Perhaps you incorrectly feel you're boasting or exaggerating.

Whatever you're feeling, just put your toe into the water now. Skim the examples below to encourage yourself. But don't copy them wholesale. You'll avoid uncovering *your* authentic, core capacities.

| honest | considerate | generous | optimistic |
|--------|-------------|----------|------------|
| loyal | well-balanced | self-sufficient | intelligent |
| capable | responsible | helpful | committed |
| imaginative | creative | willing to learn | funny |

Here's an additional way to remind yourself of your strengths: Re-visit contributions to professional and personal situations you know you've handled well or others have lauded. Again, this is not the time for modesty, especially the false kind many practice!

To capture specifics, start by writing a short, descriptive paragraph for each of about five examples. Then pull out the positive implicit or explicit qualities in your descriptions using exact words, short phrases, and insights. If you can capture any of them in a word or two, add them to your list of positive qualities.

To lay down some neural streambeds, or healthy paths of thinking in your brain for reinforcing progress, cultivate the habit of seeing yourself whole and well. Continue capturing positive information about yourself. For example, stay alert to and note in specific language examples of your positive qualities expressed in:

- experiences

- knowledge

- insights

- emotional and social intelligence

- appreciative feedback from others

- other sources and situations that show your strengths

Decide, also, how you want to capture your record of self-appreciations. Would you use a separate paper notebook, tablet, computer file, spread sheet, or index cards to help with sorting? Choose means that are easily accessible, even fun, for staying attuned to and inspired by your strengths, already expressed or budding. Include specific information such as situation, timing, and other clues to when you shine.

Maybe even do some playful drawings such as what I drew below to capture one of my moods or create ditties about what made you proud.

### *Being a goofy, wise, angelic owl who wants to use her smarts*

I hope you're having a good time acknowledging your strengths — maybe even surprising yourself with new views of your capacities. But if you continue to be inaccurately or habitually hard on yourself, you may still be a little stuck. That tends to push you downward on the see-saw of life. What good does the weight of negative emotions or self-abnegation do besides keeping you from realizing your true capacities, your courage?

Such self-denial is often expressed in an "aw shucks" misplaced, false modesty when someone compliments you. You mention, or even insist on, shortfalls or mistakes. Perhaps you attribute your accomplishments to others, luck, or a higher power. While all these influences may be present, you are still the prime actor, the person who expressed or did something. So give credit to yourself as well.

In addition to tendencies toward self-denial, do you add to or accentuate them by any of the following? Check whatever applies; add new tendencies that come to mind.

____spending time with people who use, diminish, or possibly bore you

____having significant contacts who tend to compete with you rather than appreciate, enjoy, and note your strengths

____being stuck in a culture that uses snide humor to put down others ("I was just kidding!")

____staying connected with or dependent on people who steal the spotlight from you in personal and professional situations

____discounting positive feedback by assuming sources are exaggerating or trying to butter you up

____avoiding appropriate challenges where you will stretch and learn

____embracing values and lifestyles that do not reflect or distract you from your true desires

____hinting about what you want instead of expressing it directly to people who will listen and perhaps be in a position to provide or help you get it

____devoting much of your time and energy to others' needs, ignoring most of your own important ones

____denying or downplaying your own preferences in small and important matters

____making promises you could have trouble keeping in order to please others or dodge imagined or anticipated rejection if you don't

____avoiding documenting and letting appropriate people know about your modest, typical, and significant accomplishments

If you have three or more of these tendencies, you may want to explore how you will inhibit or constrain the one that seems to limit your progress or shrivel your soul. To start, consider what elicits the response and how you might avoid the situation.

For example, remind yourself of formal and informal situations and accomplishments that offset or weaken the response. For ideas to confirm your strengths further, skim the possibilities of how to move from self-denial to self-realization listed in Table 3.2 on the next page.

What specifically will you do to begin modifying the tendency you chose within the next week? How can others help you? How will you acknowledge assistance and reward what you do?

Initially, people connected to you may be taken aback by a more confident approach that may seem to depart from their expectations. For example, I remember when I told my mother how proud I was of how I led a class. She said, "Don't break your arm." alluding to twisting my arm by verbally patting myself on the back no doubt.

Though taken aback by what seemed like a putdown, I felt some compassion for her since her generation of women had been trained to play themselves down. While I was used to both parents avoiding "spoiling" me with kudos, I nevertheless popped out with, "If I can't report on what I know I did well, who would?"

*Table 3.2*

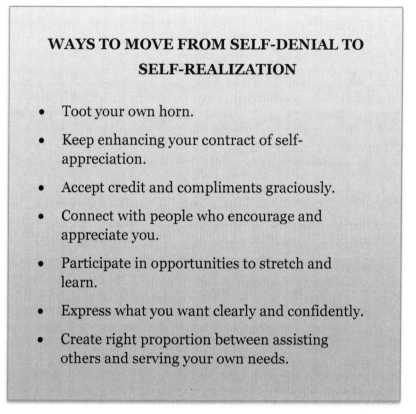

**WAYS TO MOVE FROM SELF-DENIAL TO
SELF-REALIZATION**

- Toot your own horn.

- Keep enhancing your contract of self-appreciation.

- Accept credit and compliments graciously.

- Connect with people who encourage and appreciate you.

- Participate in opportunities to stretch and learn.

- Express what you want clearly and confidently.

- Create right proportion between assisting others and serving your own needs.

After that, Mom never tried to blunt my occasional proud reporting again, perhaps realizing she had put me down. Ironically, I remember hearing reports of her discussing my accomplishments with others in what seemed exaggerated descriptions to me, as some parents tend to do!

Perhaps, you puff yourself up defensively or know of people who take such an opposite tack to self-denial, trumpeting "how great am I!"

*Image is in the public domain believed to be free to use without restriction in the US.*

Metaphorically, this can poison the atmosphere as well as connections with others as the puffer fish above actually does. More importantly, such distorted self-importance also ducks being true to oneself. Whether through exaggeration or denial, specious self-protection makes individuals opaque, inaccessible, and possibly dangerous. In turn, this tendency contributes to artificial expression, often closing the door to confident, authentic self-realization.

## Are you ready to wrestle with your negative emotions?

Complementing Tillich's idea of the tension between self-realization and self-denial, psychoanalyst, teacher, and writer Otto Rank offered useful insights. They can help with understanding small sources of discomfort or stronger emotions such as guilt, fear, or anxiety.

Rank notes the *dynamic* process, or oscillations, of development ranging from self-denial to self-realization. He recognizes the ups and downs, the stasis, the regressions, and leaps forward. To me, this view reflects a more realistic sense of how a person's development actually unfolds, versus the linear model in many books and some developmental theories. Understandably, in the search for order and predictability, many are more comfortable with such neat explanations.

In a sense, uncertain reality is mirrored in the geographic metaphor of plate tectonics and waves of earth's energy. http://www.platetectonics.com/book/page_4.asp

As tectonic plates grind against one another, results vary from extreme tsunamis and earthquakes to small rumblings. Given this tumult under the surface, the expectation of always standing on firm ground may be just as illusory as unchanging beliefs in what is true and right. Certainly strong negative emotions such as fear, anxiety, and guilt can feel as though one's very foundation is shaking. Maybe those waves of energy disrupt as well as create positive outcomes.

Rank also thought shifts in behavior reflect underlying fears of death, as well as fears of life – or having to live as an isolated individual. Fear of death can also relate to fear of failure and fear of life to fear of success, however you define failure and success, as discussed in Step One.

On a less lofty plane, the ebbs and flows among these dynamic processes can be accentuated by impulsive or reactive behaviors; they cause detours or misuse of capacities. An example can be grabbing hold of whatever comes your way instead of going to the seeming trouble of figuring out, seeking, and working for what is truly wanted. Immediate gratification and avoidance of ambiguity, or just having the security of a bird in the hand, seems preferable to the unknown—even if it may eventually contain coherence and comfort flowing from the process of becoming courageous.

Instead, let psychic muscles grow as you move in authentic directions based on goals with real meaning to you. Appropriate assistance is more likely to emerge as your own clarity encourages others to trust and respect you.

As you continue to honor who you are and what you want, your true self becomes more apparent, more realized. The hiding place of self-denial eventually collapses leaving a good foundation to build a sturdy structure for self-realization. Security is based on your very nature rather than iffy or meaningless matters.

Postpone this process and irretrievable time is lost. You'll be less prepared to deal with external stuff that may constrict you. You may even feel like a punching bag or ping pong ball bouncing in a small space designed by others. You'll know you're entering that danger zone when you continue to focus primarily on:

- what's out there only

- just what you already know about

- what others think you should do or be

- self-criticism

- overwhelming or unevaluated should-dos that burden you

- new or distracting temptations that continue to deflect your energies from authentic goals and interests

- over-extension in activities that leave little time for renewal, relaxation, and commitment to important priorities for yourself

- perfection rather than appropriate use of your time and attention to goals that reflect what you cherish

As Bruce Mau, a Canadian designer who founded The Institute without Borders, said: "keep moving away from what you know."

To take small steps in this direction, imagine you could have a future with potential for hope, fun, and meaning. A simple, concrete way to start could be sharing a stimulating experience with someone who's important to you.

Choose one or two activities for follow up from these specific examples:

- Explore fresh or different views and experiences (see www.TED.com, www.TEDx.com, www.c-span.org, www.booktv.org and www.gelconference.com)

- Apprentice yourself to or shadow someone who does work or play that excites or intrigues you; explore what you can offer in return for mutual mentoring.

- Engage in one course or experiential opportunity that you've been dreaming about for a while such as drawing, improvisation, skiing, or writing.

- Substitute a limiting habit with a new, enjoyable one.

- Make regular time for prayer or meditation.

- Be in pleasant, calm environments regularly that allow you to quiet your mind and feed your soul.

- Exchange information and assistance with individuals who have different or complementary experience and capacities.

- Cultivate some new, good relationships with people of varying ages and backgrounds who have positive attitudes toward you and themselves.

- Clarify and expand your own focus to replace indecision and distraction.

- Plan one viable adventure you will start with a few small steps this month.

- Collaborate on a project that interests you with people you like and trust.

- Deepen your patience with yourself and situations by having reasonable or just modest expectations.

- Be kind to yourself and others in your actions and interpretations.

- Find ways to show your gratitude or share your powers in order to assist others.

- Express your sense of humor and playfulness in stimulating, appropriate ways to yourself and others.

- Ask someone whose company you enjoy to join you in a mini-adventure appealing to you both.

What? You don't have the time to pursue even one of these suggestions? You can't find one or two hours a week to start something that will bring pleasure and promise?

Then ask someone who has your interest at heart to give you periodic nudges forward. Start with small steps. Avoid relying on will power alone or shoulds. Has that worked anyway?

Instead, let what makes you unique be a beginning. Uncover what's already there by slowly peeling away automatic behaviors that are not in your interest: the ones that probably bore you as well as waste time and energy. Name one now that you'd like to let go. Examples could be:

- being so polite that you blank out your true self and feelings

- using conventions such "how are you?" and going no further in connecting with others

- offering assistance when you don't have the time or interest

- keeping creative or interesting thoughts to yourself

- squelching your sense of humor or playfulness

Table 3.3 on the next page provides a listing of promising actions for pleasure and delight.

*Table 3.3*

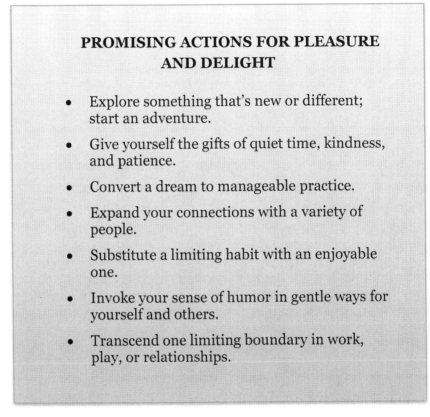

**PROMISING ACTIONS FOR PLEASURE AND DELIGHT**

- Explore something that's new or different; start an adventure.

- Give yourself the gifts of quiet time, kindness, and patience.

- Convert a dream to manageable practice.

- Expand your connections with a variety of people.

- Substitute a limiting habit with an enjoyable one.

- Invoke your sense of humor in gentle ways for yourself and others.

- Transcend one limiting boundary in work, play, or relationships.

Table 3.3 shows a listing of promising actions for pleasure and delight. A 2010 research paper supports focus on such a gentle, incremental approach to starting within yourself while moving away from what's comfortable or known. Senay, Albarracin, and Noguchi found that participants with questioning minds

> *were more intrinsically motivated... They were looking for positive inspiration from within, rather than attempting to hold themselves to a rigid standard. Those asserting will lacked this internal inspiration, which explains in part their weak commitment to future change...Those who were questioning and wondering were open-minded —*

143

*and therefore willing to see new possibilities for the days ahead.*[31]

How valuable then is the first word in the definition of how people become courageous: willingness. That shows the process opens by choosing unconditionally, voluntarily sacrificing alternatives.

Just deciding can create hope and start to mobilize your powers, as catalysts for action. Making authentic choices will help you let go of unfounded guilt that could flow from not being able to do everything or be everything to everyone. Even if you can't express exactly what you want or where you're going at a particular time, an interim choice brings several benefits:

- a feeling of relief from no longer having to deal with the blah-blah or monkey chatter within your mind

- space, energy, and time for moving forward instead of staying stuck

- enthusiasm promoting readiness for action and the possibilities that emerge

In contrast to over thinking situations, action, however inchoate itself, can contribute to peace of mind. You'll be better prepared to accept and experience any "small" deaths or seeming losses that choosing seems to bring — whether in relation to yourself, your situation, or another person.

You'll also avoid that dangerous four-letter word, *more,* which can violate useful boundaries and never specifies how much is enough. Instead, you'll be choosing what's truly valuable or at least enough for now. Over time, as you approximate or meet important goals, you'll always have the choice of returning to what appealed previously. You may even find its siren call has quieted with the passage of time.

Maybe what you let go will no longer tempt you. Or your new current experiences could have led to a different wish or interest. Or if the goal, situation, or person still entrances you, the time elapsed is a good test of its lasting value. If some *more* makes sense, then you can always return your attention to the matter, perhaps in even better circumstances and more authentic ways.

**Fly away from discomfort, fear, anxiety, and guilt**

## Free yourself to fly where and as you wish...

To encourage continuing progress and to limit negative emotions, what actions will you take based on your insights and ideas from what you've just read or learned independently? By stopping to choose one simple action to do right now, you'll help make that time count. For example, use your answers to the following as a basis for taking concrete action:

- What will I do that would be easy and worthwhile right now?

- What specific, accessible, material resource do I need to proceed?

- How will I get the resource?

- When will I take the one action?

- Who can assist me?

If nothing comes to mind immediately, maybe the following will stimulate ideas. After reading the three suggestions below, adapt and commit to one option that could make just a modest difference in your life. Schedule any related activities over the next few weeks, allowing time for manageable follow through.

- Name one source of guilt you are experiencing now. Briefly assess how credible or how useful it is to continue embracing it. What do you gain and lose by holding on to it? What one action will you take to weaken its hold?

- Describe in several sentences or less what you can do to go through one unproductive emotion by naming, claiming, and dumping its most obvious aspect.

- Identify who will help you work through one negative emotion that's holding you back from improved ease and clarity. Commit to a time within the next week to reach out to this person. What will you say? What will you offer?

As you wish, return to any aspect of this Step or previous ones you noted that inspire you or echo in your mind. They are the suggestions and ideas you're more likely to use or adapt.

In addition to choosing actions from the three sets of choices above and others that come to mind, this Step addresses one other block to progress that can accentuate discomfort, fear, anxiety, and guilt. It relates to old ingrained, often automatic associations you have that keep you mired in the past.

# Unleash yourself from early, limiting imprints

Among other creatures, baby ducklings and geese are known to treat humans as mothers if imprinted from birth. They follow such humans around, just as they would their actual mother birds. www.youtube.com/watch?v=hwOtEqulb6U&feature=related

Humans can display similar behavior based on early influences, especially when new situations remind them of primal experiences. They not only attach themselves to a person or situation, but also repeat related responses – consciously or unconsciously.

Smell, sound, and other sensual cues can unlock such memories. Similarly, an association with a past person, idea, mood, or emotion stimulates automatic behaviors. More significant or even dangerous are inappropriate choices such connections prompt. If this sounds like a familiar pattern, ask yourself whether or not an association keeps you trapped in patterns no longer suited to who you are and what you want now.

The less conscious the connection, the less likely you will be to disconnect from what influenced you previously. Since you are unaware, the imprint could freeze you in place. You'll be predisposed to feeling or acting as you always have.

One way to sneak up on an imprint is to think about unproductive patterns of behavior you may have. Perhaps explore at least one of these questions:

- What seems to spark them?

- What associations do they bring to mind?

- What repetitive, unuseful patterns do you see in your reactions and behaviors?

A catalyst that sparks your memory of a previous connection can seem pleasant such as smelling something marvelous. Or it could be something dangerous such as associating a new person with someone from your past who attracted you, but ultimately did harm. Often the connection can be to unfinished business related to what you wanted or needed. There's a hole in your soul that a parent, friend, relative, spouse, boss, colleague, lover, or situation never filled.

In my own life, confronting repetition of my poor choices are captured in this brief description which may be of use to you: Instead of dwelling on what was wrong with the previous men in my life, I finally looked within to my own complicity. Then I got another blinding glimpse of the obvious as I did with my math block.

The men either had significant characteristics and features or acted in ways that reminded me of men who were important to me in my early life: my father, an uncle, and an English teacher. I would have saved myself a lot of grief and time had I realized earlier how I'd been imprinted and by whom, how I chose echoes of what was no longer possible to re-create rather than what I truly wanted and needed now. To be kind, maybe I just wasn't ready yet.

*Table 3.4*

## HINTS THAT OLD IMPRINTS COULD BE LIMITING CURRENT PROGRESS:

- unwarranted or overly strong reactions to people or situations

- repeated, destructive, or unproductive behaviors

- expectations beyond what's possible or likely

- effort and commitment above what's appropriate

- overweening need to control or force something

- unstinting self-criticism

- impulsivity about matters that require more consideration and better judgment

- avoidance of people and situations in your interest

- dismissal of or refusal to consider well-founded guidance or suggestions

- procrastination about crucial matters

- stubborn pridefulness

Or perhaps an imprint brings an unpleasant association or assumption that you transfer forward to something that's actually different or even positive now. Table 3-4 shows hints of imprints that could be limiting your current progress. Often unproductive behavior in stressful personal and professional situations mirrors such predispositions. Maybe an aggressive or intrusive colleague threatens, angers, or scares you. Though the person's behavior might be appropriate in a professional context or just something to let pass, it rattles you due to your association with a past experience or relationship.

Even more limiting can be a hangover from a previous conception of who you are or what you should be. The comfortable or automatic habit of acting as your old self includes behaviors that remind you and others of the past.

Intensifying this are others' expectations. They may prefer your previous incarnation because it serves their interests, mutes their fears and anxieties related to change, or provides predictability.

As a result, there may not be enough oxygen left for your emerging self. For example, I remember my mother saying, "Ruth, that's not like you," commenting on something I did. I asked her, "What's like me?" That probably gave her some food for thought, but also allowed me to assert myself in an open way.

If you wish, ask yourself if you're acting "like you" are now. Think about how you could engage people close to you whom you trust in conversations about how each of you has evolved. When possible to do, that could lead to better mutual understanding and make transitions flow better for everyone.

No matter what you take away from the previous paragraphs, you may not always be able to identify clearly previous experiences or situations that keep you stuck repeating past associations and behaviors. To shake loose, consider the following situations, information in Table 3.4, and whatever else comes to mind for some leads. Some of these hints may be relevant, some not.

- when you have a reaction to a person or situation that seems stronger or more disquieting than warranted

- when you keep repeating patterns of behavior and choices that limit or hurt you

- when a person, opportunity, or object has overweening appeal or distaste to you

- when your expectations are greater than what's actually possible or reasonable

- when you push yourself beyond endurance, capabilities, time available, value of the activity, or true interests

- when the need to control or force something or someone overtakes its usefulness, benefits, or appropriateness for you and others

- when you're unnecessarily or destructively hard on yourself

- when you rush through something important or make an abrupt or impulsive decision, avoiding dealing with or accepting the messiness of ambiguity, uncomfortable feelings, and other realities

- when you avoid a person or situation that could benefit you

- when you find yourself habitually leaving particular problems or needs to the last minute, becoming unable to handle them as well as you'd like

- when you avoid keeping a promise, causing more misunderstanding than a simple acknowledgement of inability to do so ever would

- when you automatically or rudely dismiss or refuse to consider caring or insightful suggestions from trustworthy people who have your best interests at heart

- when pride, inflexible goals, perfectionism, unsupportable excuses, or self-protectiveness precludes you from accomplishing something you want

You may also find unproductive patterns and common themes in actions you regret. Once understood and you become clear in your mind about the consequences, you'll likely be better motivated to avoid repetition. Then, when you make a thoughtful choice and take one manageable step forward, positive results could start to flow better. Though you won't capture lost time, you'll be able to improve rhythms and actions for enjoying life, based on who you are and what you want now.

By now you'll appreciate that expecting only rational behavior from yourself and others is not realistic. What would be rational anyway? Is being "objective" and reasonable always the appropriate way? Given unconscious bias, is objectivity possible?

So keep attending to how negative emotions can be co-opted or worked through for your benefit. While acting as if the best outcome is possible to ensure your actions are effective, have neutral expectations about whether they will always have happy or specific results. You are unlikely to control everything, even yourself. But you do have influence and you can learn from misguided detours that really don't save and likely waste time, I believe!

# STEP FOUR:
# Surpassing Internal Barriers

*When we are no longer able to change a situation, we are challenged to change ourselves.*
Austrian neurologist, psychiatrist, and Holocaust survivor
Viktor Frankl

*Becoming courageous involves the willingness to realize your true capacities by going **through** discomfort, fear, anxiety, or suffering and taking wholehearted, responsible action.*
Definition of the process of becoming courageous from Ruth
Schimel's dissertation research

## Let's talk turkey about moving forward

Step Three focused on negative emotions such as discomfort, fear, anxiety, suffering, and guilt as well as psychological imprints from the past that influence current behavior. Suggestions offered a range of concrete ways to convert insights to action in your interests. Throughout the process, the magic of movement starts within, with your own efforts.

Step Three also described how internal barriers can actually bring opportunities when you deal with them. Then you'll be opening a door even if opportunity doesn't knock, to paraphrase comedian Milton Berle.

© *Photograph by Zeke Mekonnen*

### *Time to stop gobbling and start talking turkey ...*

This Step Four focuses further on how to know and loosen the specific habits that hold you back, the hangovers from the past that suck energy better used for effective action to benefit yourself now and later.

As possible, make the process more efficient by applying one action to address two matters. Instead of thinking in terms of doing one thing *or* another, you'll save precious time and effort. You'll also be contributing to your confidence and capacities, laying some strong, flexible cables that support bridges to the life you truly want. (More than one bridge is possible.)

As you consider the following examples which also relate to aspects of Step Three, choose one to start building a bridge. Adapt any one you choose from these suggestions as well as follow through on your own ideas.

- Explore one cause of discomfort to determine a few ways to minimize it.

- Name one major fear to figure out how to address or work around it.

- Tame or isolate one significant internal gremlin to decrease anxiety.

- Distract attention to a significant source of guilt by storing it in mothballs for at least a season.

- Unshackle yourself from a negative psychological imprint from your past that blocks blooming by substituting one positive influence from your life now.

Starting to build bridges to your future can connect to "ur" results as choreographer Twyla Tharp describes the part of her evolving creative process that starts something major. If something minor, you'd still benefit.

I know from my own experience that guidance of any kind is easier to write and read about than to apply. To promote your own action, I encourage you to choose and commit to one action that's manageable and inspiring.

Yet given your own and others' life experience and habits, you may wonder about how ideas, information, and even inspiration alone will help you transcend longstanding barriers. Remember, though, you have the mortar of your positive genetic predispositions, experiences, and external supports as resources already at hand.

But even these resources coupled with your motivation and sincerity may not suffice. Just reading another book will not magically lead to a better life. According to Marketdata Enterprises, the U.S. market for self-improvement products and services is about a $1.1 billion business. With all these tools, why should this book be worth your time, be more effective than most?

© *Photograph by Andrew Winter*

## *Move toward the light, where promising possibilities await...*

*Choose Courage* emphasizes *how to* make the most of your unique capacities, actual and dormant, by offering two complementary ways: a new, viable definition of courage that provides a road map for your action coupled with an array of tailored routes for realizing your strengths.

Given emphasis on appreciating your full self, you are not starting with a blank slate. In addition, books, workshops, exercises, therapies, and other sources you may have already tried can be incorporated as you wish. Yet despite previous solace, ideas, and guidance, would be reading this if you'd already achieved what you wanted?

The design and content of *Choose Courage* supports both your motivation and strengths. Instead of focusing on strangers' stories which populate so many self-help sources, this process:

- provides a new, accessible definition of courage, based on actual research with everyday people

- shows your capacity for courage through your own stories and actions

- offers a range of practical, concrete steps to use in sequences that work for you, since books are linear but life is rarely that neat or rational

- gives options suited to varieties of abilities, values, and reward preferences

- uses approaches such as checklists, humor, sidebars, drawings, photographs, poems, and other artful inspiration to spark positive emotions and associations

By coupling hope and vision, emotion and intellect, you'll have access to a range of nutrition suited to different situations and needs. The book design recognizes that most growth occurs over time, but not always in timely ways. Opportunities and assistance won't necessarily ride to the rescue just because of need. Yet having new tools, inspiration, and guidance will help you proceed. You'll have the reins regardless of external influences.

Whether your goals are lofty or modest, clarifying them as you proceed is important. Don't expect them to be always supported by resources, capacities, and patience. But view even disheartening shortfalls as opportunities for stretching and development — as well as for rest and recuperation.

Bottom line: While breakthroughs of understanding and insight certainly help, honesty with yourself and authentic action are keys for creating the quality of life you want. Whether nonlinear, organized, experimental, or unplanned, your choices and follow through primarily will spark the progress you want.

# Power and choice are within you

As author James Baldwin said, "There is never time in the future in which we will work out our salvation. The challenge is in the moment; the time is always now."

Improving clarity about what's important to you now will contribute to effective use of time and other resources. Equally valuable are reasonable expectations for yourself as well as people who care about and assist you. Together these two approaches will help you summon patience and focus as well as be kind to yourself and others.

Reality can bite, though. Even the best circumstances, guidance, and inspiration can't make you move, however sincere you are. So if you don't feel quite ready yet, dip briefly back into Step Two. That will show how to use your authenticity, commitment, passion, and vocation, however you wish to explore and express it.

Today, though, your responses to some of the following questions may get you in gear:

- What is the most crucial matter in your life that cries for attention right now?

- What one responsibility or need will you let go to free some time and energy to respond to that cry?

- What one major tendency or habit that holds you back will you start to tackle to permit better use of your capacities?

- How will you begin a manageable rhythm of steps for gaining the momentum to sustain attention to your chosen focus? Specify and schedule your first step.

## *Getting wiser through paying attention and action...Whooo me? Yes, you!*

Continue experimenting with promoting your progress by asking regularly: "What do I really want to do and what one step will I take to support that now?" Without such sustained focus and follow through even your best intentions can deflate, hissing like a balloon losing air.

Notice I'm not suggesting you create grand plans or change who you are and what you truly want. Instead, keep attending to your real preferences. Slowly shed the barnacles that are encrusting you, keeping you from being fluid and flexible as you choose your next steps and take action. To quote novelist and critic, Marcel Proust: "A real voyage of discovery consists not in seeking new landscapes but in having new eyes."

Your challenge and opportunity is to continue being authentic, in modest as well as more significant ways. That will build on what is unique and valuable about yourself, actually the more direct way forward. In contrast, starting from zero or imitating someone else is likely just a detour and distraction from honoring yourself.

While some of your behaviors may need regular monitoring and some modification, purpose and pleasure are more likely to emerge as you lead from your strengths and interests. Stay alert, also, to what feels like play to you, whether in work or not, what expresses your passions. Exploring those possibilities will add vibrance to your life.

To merely echo some artificial goal or another person's values, or serve someone else's needs to the exclusion of your own wastes your energy making believe. So does rebelling against the expectations of other people and society. Both can dilute what has meaning to you, what may bring other forms of lasting satisfaction and contribution. Or are conformity and rebellion forms of hideouts from pursuing what's truly wanted? For some related straight talk, read the poem in Step Two, *Dangers to Being True to Yourself.*

## Moving beyond distractions and detours

Suggestions from Step Three about marginalizing, eliminating, or converting negative thoughts and hangover imprints are not always easy to apply. They work best when you use your own good instincts, intuition, and experience. To nudge your choices and actions in inspiring directions, use this Step to make additional progress in minimizing unproductive habits and tendencies.

Who starts effective weeding habits or erases what's been in the way overnight? Sometimes, in fact, hitting bottom may be the only catalyst to force a real shift. Bouncing back from stasis, sadness, mistakes, or loss could open paths for new opportunities.

So let your survival instincts displace self-recrimination or disgust. Take small steps to reach out and open up instead of getting stuck in distractions, addictions, or homelessness, actual or symbolic.

Wherever you start, stay alert to the meaning within your current or seemingly past interests. For example, if you're interested in a sport, what aspects appeal? Is it strategy, physical power, competition, teamwork, individual merit, or some combination? When particular people or beliefs inspire you, what are the specific characteristics that attract you? What characteristics and substance in work or a relationship sustains your interest and commitment?

**Curiosity did not kill the cat. It just led it to new sources and places.**

No matter how unattainable what you admire may seem at first, peel back the layers to identify modest, specific aspects that could be more accessible. Continue to find inspiration for new behaviors and action from the underlying themes and meaning that already engage you.

Peeling back such layers can make what seems unknown less mysterious. Instead, you will feel more *curious*. And the voyage that beckons could contribute to clarity about direction and what's important in your life. As historian Henry Adams said,

"You can never tell what you want to do till you see what you have done."

Try checking out your thoughts and insights with a few people who have your true interests at heart. Without letting preconceptions or projections from their own experiences infiltrate conclusions, use a good conversation to unearth what's important. That conversation could part the curtains to a vision for the future or something much less dramatic.

At the seeming other end of the spectrum from finding and expressing your authentic vision might be a search for conventional success. Beware of some forms that can trap you, distracting from what's really important or degrading the quality of life.

That's the story of Faust: In exchange for fame and fortune he could not imagine getting on his own, he sold his soul to the Devil. Such pacts can be made consciously or unconsciously for other things too, including security, prestige, power, or even certain relationships. In fact, a 2012 article in *Scientific American Mind* discusses *The Perils of Paying for Status,* *http://www.scientificamerican.com/article.cfm?id=the-perils-of-paying-for,* reporting that recent research suggests paying more for products or services can mask a sense of powerlessness or lack of influence.

© *Drawing by Ani Bustamante*

## *This donkey man / devil gets what "he" wants.*

Knowing when decisions are based on increasing status could help break a cycle of temporary pleasure, ending in a sense of emptiness or misuse of resources for longer-run purposes — or just added stuff. When significant payments or deals are made that don't reflect values and interests, the choice is not based on true meaning. By letting go of an important part of oneself, for a possibly dangerous or unbalanced Faustian bargain, what is gained?

Many people fool themselves or postpone progress in less dramatic ways. Among my own detours have been:

- paying for training or guidance I didn't apply

- investing in collaborations that appear sensible because of complementary knowledge and skills, but lack common values, goals, commitment, and trust

- cultivating a person or joining a group for what it could get me, rather than being intrinsically interested

- lingering too long in professional and personal situations that were not good matches or diminished me

- settling for comfort and convenience rather than opening new doors to adventure, learning, or variety

- leaving something important dormant or avoiding addressing conflict so long that outcomes were sabotaged or diminished

The following Table 4.1 shows actions to avoid postponing progress.

*Table 4.1*

## ACTIONS TO AVOID POSTPONING PROGRESS

- Schedule immediate follow up when you commit to something.

- Plan and do necessary baby steps to practice new learning.

- Create viable collaborations based on common values, interests, goals, and trust.

- Join groups based on true affinity.

- Listen to intuition about letting go of personal and professional situations and connections that don't serve your interests or limit you.

- Move beyond your comfort and convenience zones.

- Organize ways to address pending projects in timely, yet incremental ways, obtaining assistance as appropriate.

- Address conflict or remove yourself from an unpromising situation.

*Table 4.2*

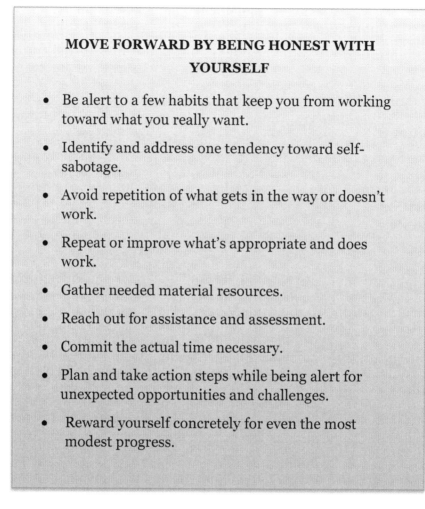

**MOVE FORWARD BY BEING HONEST WITH YOURSELF**

- Be alert to a few habits that keep you from working toward what you really want.

- Identify and address one tendency toward self-sabotage.

- Avoid repetition of what gets in the way or doesn't work.

- Repeat or improve what's appropriate and does work.

- Gather needed material resources.

- Reach out for assistance and assessment.

- Commit the actual time necessary.

- Plan and take action steps while being alert for unexpected opportunities and challenges.

- Reward yourself concretely for even the most modest progress.

Detours and hideouts from progress lose time, at the very least. Doing the opposite from them or remodeling behavior is a better choice. That's almost always possible when you do some preparation, take manageable steps, and enlist support. Patience and time are also part of this process. How can you use suggestions in Table 4.2 to move forward?

- What opportunities for converting a likely loss to a probable gain do you have in a current situation?

- If so, name one now.

- What one related step will you take this week? Do schedule it.

# Using your own keys to effective action

I believe I give my clients empathy, guidance, information, tools, and inspiration to promote their self-sufficiency. But that's not enough to meet their goals as well as to honor their true selves. As mentioned previously, the most important catalyst in their progress is within them: their willingness to be honest with themselves. No matter what I offer and how much I care about their progress, no matter the power of their vision, strengths, and motivation, they are the "magicians," not me.

Then how will you start to make your own magic? Though maybe a little uncomfortable at first, briefly describe one or two habits you have that are holding you back from being who you want to be and doing what you want to do. Rather than focus on other people or situations beyond your control, create a small window into your own mind, emotions, and heart. Assuming you have washed those panes (pun intended), some clearer views will emerge!

To assist, the previous Table 4.2 offers some suggestions and processes to encourage such honesty with yourself. In addition, adapt, choose, or save any of the leads below that have potential benefit for later use. As you wish, test your ideas with a few trusted, respected people.

For example, consider starting a small group for conversation and mutual assistance. Explore how you would agree on norms and goals for supporting and helping one another.

Processes for a mutual support group might include:

- rotated leadership and sharing of other responsibilities

- agreed-upon norms such as frankness moderated by kindness

- commitment to regular, pre-planned meetings in person, online, or via conference calls, once monthly at a minimum, with manageable agendas of three to five items

- fair use of air time, encouraging the quiet participants and providing boundaries for the very expressive ones

- food and beverages to encourage conviviality and conversation as well as to provide energy, when meeting in person

Whatever your reservations about exploring matters that hold you back, begin with something within your ken to free yourself. As an example, what about your personal appearance? Probably few people are as concerned about or alert to how you appear as you think — unless you fall considerably short of doing your appearance justice. And if they choose to judge you harshly, there's probably not much you can do about it anyway. Nevertheless, if you see possible benefits, explore how you may enhance your self-presentation in authentic, appropriate ways.

Maybe choose one or two affordable changes that make sense to you. Before starting, check out your ideas with a few people whose judgment and taste you trust. Perhaps pick up some pointers by observing people whose styles of dress and other aspects of appearance appeal. A useful book for women available for a few dollars second hand on www.amazon.com is *The Look* by Randolph Duke. There are other related books available there for men; just type in key words such as *dressing well for men* in Books.

# Questions to identify and address blocks to progress

Whether or not you want to collaborate with others on being honest with yourself about significant matters that block you, here are questions that may assist you. Although there is some logic in following the sequence, choose or adapt any that appeal to you. Most important, identify and schedule one or two important related actions your responses suggest.

- What is the main tendency that gets in the way of working toward what I want?

- What have I done about it in the past that hasn't worked or is unnecessary to repeat?

- What specifically have I done about it in the past that's been useful?

- About how much time will I commit weekly to work on this, using intuition, ingenuity, and intellect? How and when will I schedule it?

If you're still having trouble getting started, perhaps the following four considerations will provide insights to develop strategies for moving ahead. Check any that sound familiar or useful for taking action.

_____I am loath to begin something I haven't done before or don't feel capable of doing; I will take one small step into doing it by:

_____I will avoid distracting myself by obsessively thinking about matters and people I can't control by:

_____I can benefit from cultivating healthy, supportive, mutual relationships by:

_____To support my most important goal, I will develop this skill or ability _____ by:

As an example of how to move beyond a tendency that's not in your interest, let's take the issue of starting something challenging, or new. To get engaged, perhaps start a conversation with yourself. One I have had that helped me loosen up follows. Though I could also have discussed this with someone, exploring within first can be a good start that's immediately accessible.

> *If I keep doing (name what you do) over and over because I'm good at it, the repetition will eventually bore me. I could get tennis elbow of the mind! Maybe the ease and security that comes with feeling or being considered expert could even lead to inattention and less effective outcomes. So while remaining in a zone of safety and comfort helps avoid anxiety about starting something new, I actually might lose the creativity and confidence that evolves through trial and error and taking reasonable risks.*

> *I could also lose an opportunity to explore something related, new, or interesting, to add breadth or depth to what I'm doing already. Maybe I'd miss something exciting. Others would not see my potential, possibly labeling me a specialist within a silo.*

> *To avoid staying stuck in my safety first habit, I will take a few small steps. What or who will be my water wings as I wade into this river that could help me float forward (e.g. cheerleaders, knowledgeable guides, reminders of past, relevant successes, design of a simple process for enjoyment and learning, naming of my first steps)? At least I'll give exploration 30 minutes today.*

> *This week, I know I can do that for a few days. Based on what happens and how I feel about what's unfolding, I'll reconsider what to do next. But keep taking small steps and exploring, Kid (my affectionate, if inaccurate, name for myself)! Splash around.*

Whatever your main block, unproductive habit, or tendency is, have a chat with yourself about it. Stop now and just jot down a few notes to capture some themes for the chat.

At some point, though, you'll have to let go or put aside concerns about what's holding you back. Otherwise, repeating them will deepen the established neural grooves in your brain contributing to making unproductive behaviors habitual. Just as your tongue returns to cavity that needs to be filled, you'll just be returning to automatic behaviors instead of laying down a new path through your actions.

What will draw you forward now? Perhaps these suggestions for action will launch you:

- In one sentence, quickly specify what you truly want for one or two important aspects of your life. If you mention two, make one personal and one professional.

- What two to four main forces are working in your favor to support what you want? For example, consider specific qualities, skills, knowledge, situations, resources, and people.

- What two main forces are working against you that you can influence? What concrete, manageable steps will you take to weaken the strongest one?

- What first positive step will be enjoyable and manageable? Schedule it realistically.

# Getting hints of the limiting habits at hand

As playwright Samuel Becket said, "Habit is a great deadener." Avoid succumbing to the morass by specifying habits or tendencies that are not in your interest. As you name steps to let go of or minimize the most significant one or two, effective choices become clearer.

Suggestions in the previous section focused on moving through conscious habits and tendencies that hold you back. Most important, they emphasized the value of being honest with yourself, possibly using self-talk and conversations.

This section addresses specific habits of thinking and acting with more subtle or pre-conscious sources that limit possibilities. Often related to unfinished business from earlier psychological imprints and trauma, current frustrations and fears may expose them for attention.

So automatic and entrenched, they have become part of behavior patterns of everyday life. As a result, you may not yet be aware of how modifying them could improve your life as well as contribute to better outcomes for all affected.

These more automatic habits of thinking and acting appear in many situations with family, friends, and colleagues as well as acquaintances. When not made conscious and addressed, they may continue to light up like the menacing pumpkin face on the next page.

You'll also notice such habits of thinking and acting when people in groups and organizations tend toward automatic pilot, usually from fear of something new, exposing themselves, or possibly laziness. Observe, for example, individuals who:

- are disdainful of different ideas

- overpromise and under deliver

- agree when they really don't

- keep others off balance by being unpredictable

- have hidden agendas

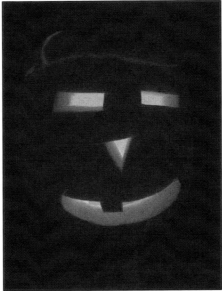

© *Photograph by Amé Solomon*

### *Imagine how you'd carve or draw a hopeful pumpkin face to encourage yourself.*

Paying attention to such themes may alert you to more effective strategies for your own situation and to improve satisfaction and productivity for anyone involved. Addressing them may multiply other opportunities for effectiveness as well.

Influencing others or shifting one of your own habits can prompt progress in unanticipated areas of your life. An example within your personal life may be developing regular sleep habits. Your health could be improved with seven to eight hours nightly. Anxiety could be lessened and energy for facing daily challenges increased. Not a bad investment.

The underlying sources of limiting habits or tendencies are not even necessary to figure out in order to break through to more effective behaviors. In addition to observation, there are indirect ways to know when you or others fall into negative patterns from the past.

Especially when you find it hard to express just what a habit may be, use the following clues to uncover a lurking one that needs attention. Check any that sound familiar.

\_\_\_\_ The intensity of a reaction, such as a need to escape, does not relate to an actual situation or person.

\_\_\_\_ People are hurt or unpleasantly surprised by something you or another person does or says.

\_\_\_\_ Something undemanding or straightforward that could be beneficial is continuously postponed.

\_\_\_\_ Feelings of resentment, dread, fear, anxiety, or helplessness seem to balloon.

\_\_\_\_ No steps are taken to address, or at least ameliorate, a destructive or dangerous situation.

\_\_\_\_ Promises are not kept, nor are affected parties alerted to lack of action.

\_\_\_\_ No constructive action is taken to relieve frustration, unhappiness, boredom, or improve a situation.

\_\_\_\_ A feeling of being overwhelmed leads to shutting down or inaction.

After reviewing any checks you made, choose the most significant one that could improve your quality of life when addressed. What situations and people seem to be involved with the matter? What themes, past and present, do you notice?

Jot down a few ideas for follow up. Then you'll be alert for signs and be ready to choose more effective action as the future unfolds.

For now, let's move to specific habits and tendencies to address. Below are examples with underlying assumptions and their negative consequences. Though they won't magically disappear once considered, you'll see a range of options for action related to the ones that affect you or others who are important to you.

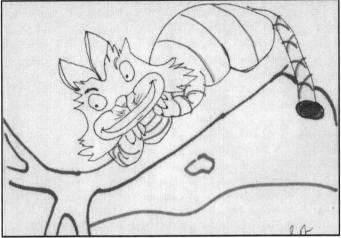

© *Drawing by Ruth Schimel*

Such awareness and consistent incremental action in your interest, married with motivation to move forward, can help you choose courage. Once you experience the new pleasures and possibilities that emerge, these hangover habits could begin to fade like the image of the Cheshire cat sitting on a branch, leaving behind only a rueful smile.

Though metamorphosis is unlikely, every small step you take helps release you from imprisonment in the past to use your true powers. As you skim through the following, decide on what relates to you or a situation you're in. Then choose how you will use, adapt, and add your own ideas.

## Specific limiting habits or tendencies and ways to transcend them

***The tendency to seek perfection:*** Perfection is expected and always a goal. Anything less is disdained, disappointing, or demeaning.

**Assumption:** Mistakes or perceived incompetence — your own and others — are negative experiences to be avoided by all means and unacceptable when they occur.

### Possible negative consequences:
- Worthwhile risks related to ambitious, new, or imaginative efforts are discouraged or avoided.

- Opportunities to learn from, correct, and transcend mistakes are missed.

- Creativity is stifled, stasis and protectiveness supported.

- Self-criticism and impatience with missing a perhaps unrealistic mark reign.

### Suggestions for moving beyond the tendency and taking action:
- Find one small project that appeals where the risk is small, but your interest relatively high. Give yourself a short, but viable, amount of time to do it. Work on it without regard to the outcome. Just immerse yourself, attending to the pleasure of the process itself. Use this approach with other projects, perhaps breaking them into digestible portions, until you grow more confident about letting go of undue expectations of yourself and others.

- Whenever you find yourself feeling worn out or losing interest from working very hard on something, ask yourself any of these questions that seem appropriate and useful:

  o What is the definition of perfection in this situation and is it possible to achieve?

  o Why is adhering to this definition necessary and useful?

- o What's the worst thing that will happen if the outcome is not perfect?

- o Will more effort or time result in a significantly better outcome?

- o How would time and energy be better used elsewhere?

- o Who will see the difference in a less than perfect result and why does that matter?

- Before you start anything worthwhile, ask yourself what amount of time is appropriate, given other priorities? Also consider the level of effort and amount of attention deserved. Perhaps use percentages such as 100, 75 and 50 to determine your degree of commitment. What other criteria would work better for you?

***The tendency to distrust others:*** People are often seen as threats or competitors. Beat others to the punch before they beat me.

***Assumption:*** Competition is the way of the world.

© *Photograph by Andrew Winter*

### *What would happen if these two beings took the risk of facing one another, willing to find opportunities together? They might protect one another or even frolic.*

*Possible negative consequences:*

- limits experimenting with a variety of approaches or expectations that could be beneficial

- squashes opportunities for collaboration and cooperation that could foster win-win outcomes

- encourages behavior that results in self-fulfilling prophecies

- exacerbates negative stress from always being on alert for threats

### Suggestions for action:

- Keep your assumptions about others in neutral until you get to know them better.

- Test a person's bona fides or trustworthiness by asking open-ended questions such as how would you handle........, what has been your experience with......, or what do you think is important in a colleague (friend, companion, etc.)?

- Engage in a low-risk effort or project to gauge the other person's behaviors.

- Check out your impressions with someone you trust.

- See the response you get when you do something generous that's no skin off your back.

## The tendency to want largess from others: People are expected to provide for your needs.

*Assumption:* Another person will make things all better.

### Possible negative consequences:

- supports passivity

- increases anxiety due to dependence

- leads to boredom from lack of challenge

- absolves assumer of taking responsibility and building confidence by strengthening skills through learning and action

### Suggestions for action:

- Whenever you assume someone else will bail you out, try helping yourself first.

- When people help you, ask or explore how you can assist them.

- Practice putting yourself in someone else's shoes, imagining their needs and wants.

- Anticipate how you could support or encourage another person and follow through.

- Check out your assumptions about expected assistance with the assumed provider.

**The tendency to believe it's not my fault:** Personal "contributions" to a problem or issue are not admitted, recognized, or explored.

**Assumption:** Only other people and situations beyond my control are to blame.

### Possible negative consequences:

- promotes passive-aggressive behavior, fault-finding, blame, defensiveness, and avoidance of responsibility

- ignores opportunities for minimizing problems through anticipating issues, mutual assistance, and the value of varied perspectives and experiences

- limits opportunities for self-development, learning, and seeing what can be contributed

- weakens connections, relationships, and trust

- decreases others' motivation to care about what happens to you

### *Suggested actions:*

- Anticipate problems or issues insofar as possible, at least planning for contingencies; do problem solving with others who could be affected.

- When something goes wrong, ask yourself first what part you may have played; this also alerts you to avoiding such problems in the future.

- Ally with people whose experience and education complement yours so that combined efforts contribute to more effective outcomes.

- Consider how avoiding responsibility affects the quality of your relationships and life.

## *The tendency to always try harder:* Doing more — and more-will solve problems, create better outcomes, and provide answers.

*Assumption:* Anything problematic or difficult can be solved by greater effort.

### *Possible negative consequences:*

- discourages distinguishing among value of pursuing something wholeheartedly, devoting some attention, and letting go

- assumes energy and time are elastic

- puts unnecessary and misplaced pressure on self and others

- militates against setting useful priorities

### *Suggested actions:*

- Regularly determine main priorities for use of time, skills, and energy.

- When you automatically push yourself or others without identifying why, assess the outcomes and value of doing that. What's a better alternative?

- Name who can assist you or to whom you can delegate some aspects.

- Have fun figuring out how to be smartly or charmingly lazy, or do less work to accomplish a similar outcome.

- Ask yourself whom you're trying to please and why that's important.

© *Photograph by Andrew Winter*

***Given how languidly adorable she is, maybe this pooch will attract someone to attend to her needs or just comfort her. Or maybe she'll just recoup her energy after resting.***

***The tendency to avoid conflict:*** Interpersonal issues, power struggles, or discomfort is to be dismissed, avoided, or escaped.

***Assumption:*** Conflict is destructive, dangerous, or bad.

***Possible negative consequences:***
- ignores advantages of conflict as a creative force for solving problems, finding common goals, ensuring better use of resources and time, and clearing up misunderstandings, among other possibilities

- energy and enjoyment are sapped by festering resentments and wasted time

- relationships fray or implode

- the dance of disconnection and dissociation continues

- benefits from managing conflict ethically, openly, and kindly are lost

### Suggested actions:
- Ask yourself what's the worst and best thing that can happen if you address the conflict. What will minimize the former and maximize the latter?

- Learn about managing conflict resolution processes; create low risk opportunities for practice.

- Observe and learn from how other people deal with conflict in useful, creative ways.

- Use a facilitator or intermediary who does not have a vested interest in the outcome or at least discuss the situation with a knowledgeable third party.

## The tendency to believe "I deserve it": A sense of entitlement is felt.

*Assumption:* Something is expected without confirmation from source or other providers.

### Possible negative consequences:
- gets others caught up in an unproductive and likely resented guessing game of trying to figure out what you want or intend

- leads to disappointment and resentment when expectations go unfulfilled or misunderstood

- does not promote shared responsibility nor strong relationships based on trust, mutual benefit, and open communication

© *Photograph by Andrew Winter*

## *This pretty parrot has all the kernels to himself. What would happen if he shared?*

### *Suggested actions:*

- Identify what you have done to deserve something — or not.

- Engage in conversations about expectations after clarifying your own to yourself.

- Avoid assuming simplistic cause and effect relationships (if I do this, then...).

- Observe how people are actually rewarded in similar situations.

- Determine what truly brings you satisfaction, materially and otherwise.

- Be specific with yourself and others, as appropriate, about what is fair recompense or exchange, tangible as well as intangible.

- Figure out if it's possible to ever get acknowledged or rewarded "adequately" for many of the things that are done (e.g. being a good parent, leader, worker, community contributor, volunteer). Do what you want to do, without expectations, appreciating whatever surprise acknowledgements you receive.

# The tendency to want to keep things as they are: Challenges and opportunities that promote useful change or growth are avoided.

**Assumptions:** Change is unlikely or not worth the effort. But even if possible, a new situation would be just too threatening or hard.

### Possible negative consequences:
- perpetuates the status quo, predictable, or rigid arrangements
- kills hope as well as squashes curiosity and creativity
- keeps individuals from discovering, developing, and demonstrating abilities
- discourages learning that could bring better results for all involved
- becomes self-fulfilling prophecy, prompting behavior that supports expectations
- leads to boredom from predictability and repetition
- avoids preparation for inevitable change

### Suggestions for action:
- Read stories, biographies, autobiographies, and articles about inspiring people who have overcome obstacles.

- Recall what has happened in your own experience when something unexpected, yet positive, occurred due to fresh or imaginative influences.

© *Photograph by Andrew Winter*

### *All the predictable, connected houses in a row just have color for differentiation. What opportunity for expansion and creativity do they offer?*

- Experiment with making one small shift toward something better.

- Find reasons why something can be done whenever you find yourself coming up with reasons why something can't be done.

- Ask yourself what would be lost by trying to improve a situation, even in modest ways.

© *Photograph by Andrew Winter*

### *"I cut up fish, using my tools and experience just as I wish, day after day."*

***The tendency to control:*** No one else could do it better, would do it at all, or should do it.

> ***Assumption:*** Everything is my responsibility. No one else knows what I know or can do what I can do.

***Possible negative consequences:***
- leads to being overwhelmed and tired from endless "to-dos"

- precludes others from doing their part and developing capacities

- frustrates and disillusions due to lack of appreciation and compliance

- misses refreshing opportunities from learning, delegation, and experimentation

- results in inauthentic relationships and resentments, expressed and not

- eats away at valuable relationships, unraveling them over time

- sends a message that there is one best way, even though it may not be sustainable and resilient enough for changing circumstances

### *Suggestions for action:*

- Explore what you gain and lose by keeping the reins exclusively in your hands.

- Ask others what they would like to do to contribute.

- Provide useful guidance to help others learn how to do what you do; "pay it forward."

- Observe how alternative ways to do things can result in acceptable outcomes.

- Describe what you're holding on to and why to yourself and perhaps to others.

- Establish quality control processes for early identification of problems and issues by everyone involved.

- Experiment with open communication about festering problems and issues.

- Be honest with yourself about your own role in the issue and what you're willing to do about it.

- Name what being freed from the tendency will allow you to be and do.

***The tendency to assume merit is the main criterion for recognition and appreciation.*** Fair treatment and remuneration should be based on merit, not politics or favoritism.

***Assumption:*** Doing good or outstanding work deserves acknowledgment and reward, commensurate with accomplishment or value.

### Possible negative consequences:

- leaves even effective producers disheartened and possibly resentful, when expectations of appreciation and recognition are unmet

- confidence and motivation are weakened by political games, so often part of reality

- disillusionment dilutes commitment in the present and future

- experience and satisfaction from making ideas or accomplishments not availed

- worthwhile informal and nonconventional knowledge and processes are lost when only merit-based outcomes are preferred

- cooperation and collaboration among people with different capacities, styles, experiences, and interests are discouraged

- attention to clashes of values are avoided or not addressed

- apolitical actors are sucked into games of manipulation and use of power alone

### *Suggestions for action:*

- Keep a record of special accomplishments, including what you did and how as a reality test; share it as appropriate in current or future situations.

- Engage in conversations, exchanging information regularly about mutual efforts.

- Ask yourself if you're doing something for intrinsic satisfaction or just pats on the back.

- Seek situations, friends, and colleagues who are willing to acknowledge one another's value and accomplishments in meaningful ways.

- Identify what kind of recompense, tangible and intangible, is important to you; choose situations where what you want is possible to receive; make expectations clear to others.

- Be alert to the typical politics inherent in many situations and how you can influence them for mutual benefit.

- Learn enough of the political game to do well.

- Choose or promote arrangements where values in common are likely to be honored.

## *The tendency to be the Lone Ranger:* Assistance is not requested or is resisted when offered.

*Assumption:* Asking for and accepting help indicates weakness and creates obligation.

### *Possible negative consequences:*

191

- People who offer assistance feel rejected, detached, or unappreciated.

- Contributions that are needed or at least could enhance what is being done go unexplored.

- The mutual benefits and enjoyment of collaboration are unavailable.

© *Photograph by Zeke Mekonnen*

### The ostrich continues on its often self-protective, sometimes aggressive way.

### Suggestions for action:

- Remember that even the Lone Ranger had a trusty sidekick, Tonto (so badly named, unfortunately); identify who you want by your side, especially someone whose strengths complement yours. There can be more than one person.

- Cultivate other colleagues and friends you respect enough to want and encourage their contributions.

192

- Explore what you'd gain by not doing everything yourself.

- Dig under your resistance to assistance to figure out what's holding you back from accepting it.

- Work on an engaging project which will benefit from combined efforts in order to experience the pleasures, and natural, but different frustrations, of cooperation.

- Learn about group dynamics so you can appreciate how to make them work for you, and support your goals, in ethical ways.

## *The tendency to believe "I'm the boss.":* Don't question my authority, ideas, or actions.

*Assumption:* someone who questions me doesn't understand the complexity of the issues or situation, nor how important my role is. Furthermore, they can't imagine what I've gone through to learn what I know and earn what I do.

### *Possible negative consequences:*
- precludes constructive exchange and exploration of possibilities beyond own ideas and style

- puts relationships in a one-down format rather than promote productive patterns based on equality and mutuality

- discourages learning from others

- thwarts shared responsibility

- wearies and perhaps bores from shouldering so much responsibility over time

© *Photograph by Zeke Mekonnen*

## *"I roar my authority with assertive nonverbal communication and other means."*

### *Possible negative consequences:*

- precludes constructive exchange and exploration of possibilities beyond my own ideas and style

- puts relationships in a one-down format rather than promote productive patterns based on equality and mutuality

- discourages learning from others

- thwarts shared responsibility

- wearies and perhaps bores you from shouldering so much responsibility over time

### *Suggestions for action:*

- Explore using other types of power besides authority and punishment for possibly more graceful, productive, creative outcomes. They include expert, reward, and referent (inspirational) power.

- See what would happen to you and others if you let go of appropriate aspects of your authority — in regard to one situation that does not involve major risk.

- Identify and study positive models of alternative behaviors. What appeals to you about them? Which one would you try now?

- Consider the benefits and risks in loosening some control through observing others as well as re-visiting examples from your own past.

After noting these tendencies, you can see more concretely how such habits of thinking and action could limit progress and possibilities for yourself and others. For any situations that apply to or seem related to your situation, use the suggestions for action that make sense to you. Adapt them and create others. Choose one to try within the next week.

## Additional guidance for moving forward

If you wish, you can analyze the reasons behind limiting habits you have at another time, perhaps with professional assistance. The focus now, though, is to imagine what you can and will do to move beyond them and encourage others to do so. As you proceed, continue to be alert to signs of potential trouble and hints of unfinished business that will result in pouring progress down the drain.

© *Photograph by Andrew Winter*

> *Pipes under sinks go to who knows where.*
> *Metaphorically, they can suck away valuable*
> *possibilities with just a glug, glug. So take positive*
> *steps forward rather than let resources and time*
> *swirl away automatically.*

Without actually taking action to transcend such blocks to a better life, you may be trapped in a confining web you don't want. To help you bring together the small steps mentioned previously that make sense to you, consider and improve on the following suggestions to make them suit your style and situation. Use and adapt any you wish.

***Name your emotions when you feel stymied or are avoiding something of value.*** At least name to yourself, the specific emotions you are feeling in the moment. Then take about five minutes — which is probably all you need — to think of other situations that have summoned the same emotions. What tendencies or patterns emerge? For additional perspective on how you want to proceed, revisit these insights later when that makes sense.

***Make some time to compose yourself and seek insight when communicating with someone.*** Take or request a few moments to think and gather your thoughts. If appropriate, excuse yourself for a short time, saying when you will return. Maybe take a few deep, slow breaths. Remember whatever comes to mind to consider later.

***Perhaps say what you are thinking at the moment, even if it feels a little uncomfortable.*** When you are in a relatively safe situation, taking this risk can open up conversation and start to build trust as well as comfort with a new behavior. Just make sure you express your thoughts in a way that does not inappropriately expose your vulnerabilities or hurt someone. Attend to the other person's reaction and address it to avoid misunderstandings or confirm common perceptions.

***Figure out what happened to continue learning.*** Revisit as specifically as possible what just occurred, including content, impressions, and images. Observe the rerun as if you had a movie in your mind. Jot down a few ideas about what you felt, what someone else did, and how you acted. Review your notes and pertinent memories to identify themes.

If you wish to go deeper, explore the people and situations from your past that seem related. What patterns do you notice in past experience that seem similar to the present one?

***Walk yourself through alternative, preferred behaviors.*** You can't change what someone else does nor erase anyone's feelings. But you could re-train yourself and expand options by creating a brief menu of ways to think and act more effectively.

To practice, do some role-playing in your mind or in person with someone you trust. As you wish, record it to hear new ways of expressing yourself. Acknowledge all aspects that are effective while choosing one or two to practice improving.

***Pat yourself on the back as you move forward.*** You may not be immediately successful in becoming aware of what is happening and modifying your behavior in your interests. In any event, acknowledge anything you do that departs from tendencies that limit your quality of life or thwart you. Find ways to laugh at foibles without being hard on yourself. Then move on to the next opportunity.

***Use mantras and phrases to ease yourself into a better frame of mind.***
Avoid beating yourself up. Instead, ask "What can I learn from this?" Adopt or create a series of ways to focus positively such as:

- Remind yourself this too will pass.

- Be persistent about promoting good outcomes.

- Listen to your intuition.

- Remember how you successfully worked through something related.

- Watch and learn from useful role models.

- Use a productive distraction from a difficulty.

***Experiment by modifying your behavior with someone affected by it who also cares about you and your development.*** When you feel it's timely and helpful, mention a behavior you'd like to change. You could say something like: "I know when I _____, it's not useful. I'm working on becoming aware of why and when this happens so I can stop from contributing to or at least minimize a negative effect. I mention this because I sense it hurts our relationship (or work) and possibly your feelings. Please make whatever comments and suggestions you have about this."

Then listen very carefully. Paraphrase what the person said to make sure you understand the response and reassure the other person you heard accurately. In extreme or highly problematic situations, consider using a third party as a facilitator.

***Be alert to even currently good habits that become deadening and unproductive with repetition.*** Many ways of doing things that start usefully can result in neutral or eventually negative outcomes. For example, always asking for assistance or explanations could give the impression that you are still a beginner far after you've developed experience and expertise. Another example is gathering information galore to figure something out, over thinking a matter, or spending excessive time refining a product or process. Those choices can just postpone focused, productive action that moves matters forward.

## Take the last word.

Now that you've had a chance to consider productive, low-risk ways to transcend unproductive habits of thinking and acting, what do you want to do?

Maybe you've already thought of one action from the suggestions provided in this Step or developed your own approach. To serve your interests, do one thing you wish to avoid losing motivation and inspiration.

Finally, use this Step to understand and possibly influence other people's behavior by being an effective role model. Just as in your own case, what seems irrational, unproductive, or inappropriate may very well have sources in earlier life and experiences. You don't need to know those sources, though, to have compassion for another person or yourself.

# STEP FIVE:
# Expressing Your Own Courage

## Becoming Courageous

*Continuous effort - not strength or intelligence - is the key to unlocking our potential.*
British Prime Minister, Winston Churchill

*Courage is rightly esteemed the first of human qualities... because it is the quality which guarantees all others.*
British Prime Minister, Winston Churchill

*Becoming courageous involves the willingness to realize your true capacities by going **through** discomfort, fear, anxiety or suffering and taking wholehearted, responsible action.*
Definition of the process of becoming courageous
from Ruth Schimel's dissertation research

Heroes who capture terrorists or brave a burning building to save victims seem the essence of courage. But how do these acts relate to you? Can you imagine doing them? Would you ever be in such a situation?

Whether or not you can see yourself in similar situations or doing other courageous acts, take heart! This Step Five will help you access your own courage in more likely, even daily, situations. You will also find ways to encourage others.

The current 187 million or so entries for courage on Google may put the word in danger of becoming a heroic cliché. Despite such extensive uses of the word, I wonder how many people have explored exactly what courage is. Without that understanding, how could you and I understand how to access and express our courage?

Just learning about others' ideas, experiences, and stories alone does not unlock how *you* can be courageous. Engage with this Step as well as other parts of this book that relate to you to see how to make the familiar, yet seemingly mysterious, capacity for courage your own.

© *Photograph by Andrew Winter*

### Paddling into what seems unknown, without a clear destination, at least starts your search process.

Novelist Ernest Hemingway's view of courage as grace under pressure is an example of romantic, but vague, definitions that abound. They provide little concrete guidance about how to develop courage — let alone, how to connect with your own. Other efforts offer possibly inaccessible examples or portray dramatic acts during warfare. They have little to do with everyday life.

Most self-help books tell stories about other people. Maybe inspiring and entertaining to readers, that approach may not help you access your own courage. They might even discourage you because you cannot imagine yourself walking in others' boots. In contrast, *Choose Courage* is a how-to-book that concentrates on what you can do to express your unique brand of courage. The process flows from the accessible definition based on actual research.

Too often, typical examples of courage are expressed in seemingly superhuman and sterling acts that stamp a person forever. Other definitions consider it a character trait available only to people with particular talents, training, and other advantages. Courage therefore seems external to you, dramatic and possibly foreign, fogging your view of your own innate capacity.

You already have insights and experiences related to your strengths and possibilities, from this book and elsewhere. The ideas, guidance, and suggestions here show the true nature of courage as a continuing process of development that can be learned by most people. Yet, the comforting illusion that you can be once and for all courageous will fade like the Cheshire cat in Alice in Wonderland. Instead, you can make the remaining cat's smile flourish again into a full-bodied version of your truer self as you replenish yourself for taking action.

© *Photograph by Zeke Mekonnen*

***As Little Orphan Annie sings, "The sun will come out tomorrow." That reality offers hope, clarity, and possibilities. Your innate courage helps all three rise.***

Does this process seem too much to deal with all the time? Well, as a member of our fallible, amazing species who could always be courageous, or even keep total focus on self-development?

In fact, striving all the time may lead to the reverse of what you seek: burnout and distorted priorities. Alternatively, experiment with widening your repertoire to include a range of rhythms, from rest to play to work.

As you vary and stretch through refreshing, engaging activities, you'll feel new energy. Benefits could reinforce one another, especially since courage sparks other strengths, as Winston Churchill said in the quote at the start of this Step.

First, you'll add to your self-respect. By acting from authentic, responsible conviction you're unlikely to lose, whatever the outcome. Simple to complex steps are confirming. They can range from expressing yourself honestly to something more significant, such as starting a project with meaning to you that requires sustained effort.

Secondly, as you gain experience and confidence in expressing your true self, continuing challenges become somewhat easier. It's like becoming adept at a new sport. At first you may feel a little clumsy. But you develop strength, coordination, aerobic capacity, and sureness with learning and practice. Pleasure in performance increases. Your staying power and timing improve. You feel stronger, more encouraged when you're hitting the mark. And when you miss, you refocus your efforts faster — especially when you don't berate yourself about it. You have the choice to continue enriching your repertoire from new learning and experience.

Third, as you continue to uncover your real range and depth, you will create better matches in work, relationships, play, and other important aspects of your life. Using your true voice will help you express what you want more clearly. You will know better what to seek, what to let go. Since you know better what you want, you can decide what is important to do. You will use your precious time more effectively. And others will find it easier to assist you because they understand what you want and trust you.

With the experience you've gained in dealing with limiting tendencies on your own and from guidance in Steps Three and Four, you'll also be diminishing such confining habits as:

- having unduly high or low expectations

- being hard on yourself

- finding reasons why important things cannot be done

- focusing on the bottom line at the expense of attending to the value of the process

- avoiding useful action because of negative feelings or psychological imprints from the past

With increasing clarity about priorities and experience demonstrating your strengths, you'll continue taking appropriate risks. You'll enter new and more satisfying cycles of accomplishment. The process of developing your courage may not lead to consistent and predictable outcomes. There could be zigzags and even regressions, but you'll be likely to move through difficulties faster with more ease, balance, and humor.

© *Art by Ani Bustamante*

***If you think the possibilities for expressing your courage are "udderly" unlikely, remember your first source of nourishment is yourself.***

Finally, as your awareness, authenticity, and accomplishments increase, life becomes richer, more interesting, and healthier. Natural issues of living tend to be catalysts rather than frustrating walls. You will be stimulated by genuine challenges instead of sidetracked with stale problems and distracting detours, with the tyranny of shoulds and poignancy of might-have-beens. As your energy flows from your true center, you will be more effective and efficient. You will feel vital – most of the time.

These promises for your progress may seem over the top. Yet you'll see in the explorations of what courage means and the proof of your capacity below, that the potential to keep them exists.

## Merging the Meanings of Courage from the Past

Understanding what courage really is can begin with considering ideas from the past that open fresh ways to appreciate it and yourself. The myth of the hero itself holds clues. As you've probably already know, confronting others and the forces of evil or nature are often cited as parts of the hero's journey.

The actual struggle starts within you. Most students of the process of heroic action agree on this, whether psychologist Otto Rank, writer and photographer Dorothy Norman, or mythologist Joseph Campbell.

© *Art by Ani Bustamante*

## *Whatever monsters menace, powers for addressing them are within you.*

You'll see the theme borne out in many engaging stories: almost any frank autobiography, well-researched history, and probing biography as well as many novels and films. As examples, consider the adventures of Harry Potter and Frodo from the Lord of the Rings. Explore Ron Chernow's recent biography of George Washington or Gordon Wood's *Revolutionary Characters: What Made the Founders Different.* Or read the stories of African American migrations from the South: *The Warmth of Other Suns* by Isabel Wilkerson.

Going further back to the start of recorded exploration of the self are insights from Stoic philosophers such as Parmenides, Zeno, and the Atomists of Pre-Socratic Greece. Such early explorers moved from making sense of the external world through time-honored storytelling to awareness of what went on inside their own minds. In one of the dialogues Socrates supposedly asked, "What is courage?"

Plato reported the conversation between Socrates and his student, allowing the reader to discover the complexity of the subject through the questions and answers. As with many important matters, nothing definitive, easy, or neat emerged. Instead the Socratic dialogue captured the struggle for clarity and understanding within the mind and through exchanges with another person.

Looking for clues in acts of courage just as modern women and men do, Aristotle identified an ethical dimension. He believed a courageous act must not only have a noble end, but also that the means must be reasoned out and executed thoughtfully. This focus on consciousness of ends and means complements more current insights that the important struggle is within the person. The process of choosing courage therefore requires reflection and responsibility.

This theme is also found in the writings of medieval philosopher-theologian Thomas Aquinas. He thought courage is related to fortitude. Like the Greeks, he considered strength of mind crucial, especially that which allows one to endure adversity or pain.

From all this you might conclude that today's focus on a dramatic act as a badge of courage misleads. That's because physical daring is only the show-and-tell part. Yet if this is so, how should the traditional epitome of courage, the soldier in battle, be seen?

The 19th century expert on war, von Clausewitz, said that courage is first among all moral virtues in facing danger. And moral courage is "the courage before responsibility, whether it is before the judgment seat of external authority or of the inner power, conscience." For von Clausewitz acting courageously is the capacity to do battle with both external and internal authority; it is the "feeling of one's own power." [32] Significantly, the philosopher of war joins respected thinkers who confirm the importance of the internal process.

To capture the deeper meaning of courage for you today, let's turn to the derivation of the word courage itself.

## The Derivation of the Word Exposes Your Courage Within

The Latin *cor* means heart. In medieval English, *corage* meant the heart as the seat of feeling. So the center of courage is heart, in

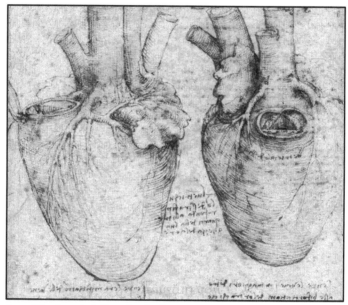

*Image is in the public domain believed to be free to use without restriction in the US.*

*Drawn by Leonardo DaVinci, 15th century*

### The rich muscularity of the heart and its blood vessels, Renaissance style

terms of word derivation and likely in practice. Echoing the established themes of courage as an internal process of development, the word itself takes us into the core of the person.

By focusing literally on the heart of courage, crucial insights emerge. Besides its anatomical meaning, heart is "the vital center of one's being, emotions, and sensibilities; the seat or repository of the emotions." [33]

Heart can then be associated with the capacity for sympathy, compassion, or generosity. People with heart have inner strength or character and fortitude, to return to Aquinas' view. A person considered lovable or loyal is a dear heart. The heart of a problem means its essence. Heartfelt comes from the very core.

Another aspect becomes apparent in the word hearty: complete, exuberant, unequivocal, and vigorous. Yet when someone wears his heart on his sleeve he is vulnerable and open, the seeming antithesis of the brave warrior.

Taken together, the meaning of courage lies in a paradoxical web of ideas. The rich connections include:

- emotional vulnerability

- character development

- compassion

- energy

- wholeness

- inner strength

- emotional vulnerability

- responsibility

- vitality

On the surface, the aggressive, bold, external manifestations often associated with courageous acts do not seem to reside comfortably with these underlying meanings.

Yet they do. Consider receptivity and assertion, vulnerability and strength, as co-existing and the complex weave of the word becomes apparent.

The paradoxes embedded in the meaning of courage also explain why there has been so much difficulty over the centuries in understanding the real nature of courage. The search for logic, clarity, and concreteness alone leads astray.

By just observing results, people have often assumed that courage is expressed in acts of derring-do or other brave behavior. But these acts merely reflect the outer process. Since that crucial internal process has not been apparent and clarified, courage can seem unattainable, however inspiring and continuously mentioned it is.

The mystery can therefore become accessible by integrating ideas of respected thinkers from a range of disciplines with the rich meaning of the word, courage, itself. The process of choosing courage involves being aware of your inner self and probing your powers. At the foundation is the word itself: the essential element of brave acts and tough mindedness is heart.

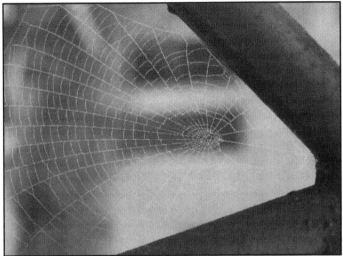

© *Photograph by Andrew Winter*

### *Just as what seems fragile in a spider's silken web is actually as strong as high alloy steel, your capacity for courage provides a powerful, if subtle, support for your action.*

The nature of this vital center of courage is found in openness to experience, emotion, and compassion. Strength can emerge from the willingness to leave space and permit quietude rather than jump to impulsive or immediate action.

In other words, starting with an open heart and mind can allow the complexity and true meaning of courage to come alive. As British actor Bill Nighy says about his colleague actor Judi Dench: "She comes unarmed. She has no shtick. She is deeply present."

Sense and sensibility, heart and head may now work together to invoke the richness of your potential and powers. Developing your capacity for courage can involve being less encumbered, less concerned with forcing an outcome. Instead, you remain receptive and ready to act authentically — from the heart, or inside out.

213

# Look Behind the Act to What Occurs Within Individuals

Whatever your age, does this 52-year-old woman sound at all familiar? "I had to learn who I was. You have to go through the pain I've discovered too. You have to fail, you have to make mistakes to learn and grow and have a better appreciation of what life is all about."

Here is a man of 34: "I recently discovered I have a singing voice, a hidden talent which I never dreamed. Not in a million years. And there it is. I joined this group because someone in the congregation encouraged me to, someone who heard me sing."

As these two mini-stories imply, blooming can involve many cycles and branches of growth, iterations of experience. It includes developing intuition, judgment, and insight from trial and error. It also involves seeking assistance and accepting good guidance as a basis for flourishing.

That's captured metaphorically in the jewel-like tree of life by Ecuadorian artists Xiomara Navas and Horacio Rubio on the next page. The foundation or roots of the tree have developed over time and are hidden from view. The branches emerging above are full of dancing lights from their gems.

Traditionally, the search for understanding often starts with stories of people's descriptions of how they deal with challenging or difficult situations, whether their actions seem conventionally heroic or not. With this in mind, be alert to how individuals you know or hear about work through conflict with loved ones and people in power.

## *"Blooming can involve many cycles and branches of growth."*

But don't get too distracted by other people's stories, unless you can imagine yourself at the center of them. Instead, come closer to home. Catch the echoes of courage in your own daily choices. Revisit the seemingly ordinary, sometimes tortuous steps you took to work through something difficult. And notice how you address situations that threaten your security and stability. Then you will probably find out how you have already gone about demonstrating your capacity for courage — or postponed doing so.

# Cultivate Openness

Your strengths, capped by courageous action, will emerge from such willingness to remain open and be vulnerable. In other words, just as you begin to feel uncomfortable in a situation and want to flee is when you probably need to stay put. Listen to yourself and others. Say what you mean and do what you say, as Dr. Seuss' Horton the Elephant would say.

To develop this willingness, it's useful to leave some space in your mind, heart, and life, time for ideas and feelings to emerge. Make opportunities to explore and experiment. Then you're more likely to get clearer about who you are now and who you want to be. This aspect of choosing courage involves *not* always taking action, *not* filling every minute of life with activity.

Yet when you allow for introspection, you may also feel as though a void looms. You could disappear down a rabbit hole or discover something unpleasant. The lack of clarity or feeling of disorientation possibly produces some anxiety.

© *Photograph by Zeke Mekonnen*

### *Notice the more mature, wiser elephant taking its time at the right, eyes open.*

You're not sure of what to do. Or you don't know how to do something or what will happen. Such ambiguity feels disquieting, even oppressive.

If that's your situation, I hope you'll remember and use your own strengths as well as cultivate the ideas and suggestions in Steps Three and Four. By using this book and other sources, you're already prepared to harvest a better outcome for yourself. Realizing that can provide patience to go through short-term discomfort as you move toward appropriate, responsible action. Your true voice and preferences will begin to emerge from what may seem vague or empty.

To support your momentum, reach for faith that the seeming unknown will eventually give way to clarity. As you do what is appropriate, your real capacities and preferences in life will continue emerging.

In the process, keep acknowledging and developing your authentic strengths by taking regular baby steps toward interim progress. If you wish, also explore the range of options for action in Step One. In the process of doing whatever you choose, intangibles such as vitality, imagination, and hope will combine with your tangible skills and abilities. You'll revel in appreciating your courage.

## Courage Defined

Integrating the ideas and guidance throughout the Steps into a definition, you can see more directly why the process of choosing courage involves:

- the willingness to realize your true capacities

- by going *through* discomfort, fear, anxiety, or suffering

- and taking wholehearted, responsible action.

Woven into the definition are emotional, intellectual, spiritual, and ethical themes. For example, the intellectual component involves knowing what is true or real and how that relates to understanding issues and solving problems. Possibly allied with Stephen Colbert's "truthiness," you may want to visit: http://en.wikipedia.org/wiki/Truthiness

The spiritual aspect of courage lies in reaching beyond the concrete by being willing and wholehearted. Ethics connect with responsibility. And the emotional is clear in references to negative emotions such as discomfort, fear, anxiety, and suffering.

For additional clarity, here are specific explanations of how each word in the definition of courage is meant:

**Willingness** is the process of choosing unconditionally, voluntarily sacrificing alternatives.

**Realize** is to comprehend fully or correctly, to actualize or achieve.

**True** is consistent with reality, genuine, fundamental.

**Capacity** is the ability to hold, do, receive, or absorb; the maximum or optimum amount that can be achieved; the ability to learn or retain knowledge; a faculty or aptitude.

**Wholehearted** is to undertake fully with sincerity, openness to experience, compassion, and energy. It is something done for itself, not as a means to an end.

**Responsible** is being ethically accountable, accepting authorship.

**Action** is the process of doing, the transmission of energy, force, or influence as the result of responsible thought and intuition.

**Discomfort** is mental or bodily distress.

**Anxiety** is the state of unease and distress about future uncertainties, lacking an unambiguous cause or specific threat.

**Fear** is the feeling of alarm or disquiet caused by the expectation of specific danger, pain, or disaster.

**Suffering** is the feeling of actual pain or distress, sustaining of loss, injury, harm, or punishment; the enduring of evil, injury, pain, or death.

This process of being willing to realize your true capacities by going through discomfort, fear, anxiety, or suffering and taking wholehearted, responsible action provides access to your actual and potential strengths. They are the skills and abilities you need to create a meaningful, rich life.

Whatever time you have ahead of you, only the present is within your grasp. Then what better time than now to renew your appreciation of yourself and build on strengths, to make your courage accessible?

Will things "happen" to you or will you take the initiative? Will you choose to be who you want to be and do what you want to do in the range of small and larger ways that daily life offers?

By seeking to express yourself accurately and optimistically, you are likely to serve your own needs better as well as make contributions to others. With that can come deep joy and modest delights.

John Donne captures connections with the whole in his poem:

*"No Man is an island entire of itself; every man is a piece of the continent, a part of the main. If a clod be washed away by the sea, Europe is the less, as well as if a promontory were, as well as if a manor of thy friend's or of thine own were: any*

*man's death diminishes me, because I am involved
in mankind, and therefore never send to know for
whom the bells tolls; it tolls for thee."*

Since action is key to realizing your capacity for courage to serve others as well as yourself, your time is now. What are the small steps you can start to take to make your time count?

## How to Start?

Attend to *how* a range of worthwhile acts unfold, the choices, struggles, and experiences that lead to what seems instantaneous. Use and build bridges to making the transitions you really want.

Examples are:

- moving through negative emotions to start something modest or ambitious, yet worthwhile
- caring for others under demanding circumstances
- dealing honestly and concretely with personal and professional problems
- learning and using any new or better ways to see and do things

Besides noticing confirmations of your own courage as you review such experiences and others that relate, what can you do to continue realizing your capacity for courage?

The good news is that there are almost as many ways to move forward as situations offer and you create. You'll always have access to your unique rhythms, skills and values, possibilities, preferences, and passions. In other words, to paraphrase the somewhat dated, but still appealing, Prego spaghetti ad, it's all within you. http://www.youtube.com/watch?v=Z3CRoyrs5rQ

Remind yourself of what you've learned about your choices and strengths from sources such as *Choose Courage* and what you know in your own heart and mind. Open doors to new information and intuitions by reminding yourself of how you've handled any challenge and difficulty, small or big.

In fact, right now, just jot down one paragraph related to the bullets above or another relevant matter you struggled through to a good enough outcome. Or capture your own words through a recording or using Dragon Naturally Speaking software, if you have it. That process will likely take less than 15 minutes.

Another approach is to move into action mode about something you value within the next few days. Start at either or both ends of a spectrum. Begin with what you love and/or what you fear. Whatever you decide, though, start gently and recognize that initial experiences might have to be repeated several times before they yield a benefit — and you and others become comfortable with what develops.

In addition to adapting or applying the ideas in previous Steps throughout the book, make one choice from among the following:

- Engage in one manageable activity every week that relates to a dream you've always pined to bring to life.

- Identify something you admire in a person you sense is also present in yourself.

- Name one characteristic in a hero of yours that you share or can develop.

- Be alert for one or two intriguing people as you participate in activities of groups and organizations. Make a connection with the person, if only to start a conversation.

- Do one easy thing that's new and appealing each week.

Over time, you'll improve daily rhythms and integrate information that strengthens your willingness to act. As you feel ready or at least curious enough to take each small step forward, continue choosing something that takes you beyond what's entirely comfortable.

In fact, discomfort can be a sign that something is worth your attention and time. What comes to mind right now for enriching your current self or sending out a new shoot related to your passion and potential?

Or maybe you don't feel ready yet for a more ambitious voyage. You don't have a clear idea of what truly engages you. One option is to keep scanning what's around you. Or maybe one of the following will get you going:

- Read an article or search online for information you'd typically ignore, being alert to any aspect you want to explore a bit further. For example, if you generally gravitate to mysteries, romance novels, science, or World War II books, try psychology, health, or historical novels. Note the patterns of any new selections and their themes that continue to intrigue you. Use that information to direct your next step, whether for learning, play, conversation, or work.

- Get to know people who seem enthralled by their interests and lurk a little in their lives.

- Take one short, hands-on workshop or listen to a talk about anything that sparks your interest or conflicts with what you believe.

- Volunteer to do something that stretches you a bit or that you would not ordinarily consider.

- Engage in conversation with someone you haven't met before or just know casually.

If you wish, also ask people with empathy, insight, and imagination who don't have an agenda for you about their ideas for topics or issues. See what they suggest you'd enjoy exploring. Encourage them to avoid neat categories and labels in favor of short descriptions of subjects, issues, and activities. Offer to assist them in their own explorations as well. Maybe you'll discover a small adventure to share.

While peering through windows and opening doors, experiment and pay attention to whatever arouses your curiosity or find ways to prompt it. Remember anything new may seem foreign and somewhat inaccessible at first. To become more at ease, make some time to lean further in. Avoid harsh self-judgment and perfectionism. Instead applaud any progress.

Finally, another approach is to tend your own backyard. Think about the quality of your important relationships. What specific actions might improve them? What one or two matters need to be addressed or changed that relate to your own behavior where you do have some influence? Ask people you trust if nothing comes to mind right now.

### *Will you walk through a new door now or explore a bit by at least peering through a window?*

Also consider the work you do and how you do it, whether paid or not. What would you want to explore if you're no longer surprised, engaged, or challenged enough?

- What new or related subjects, skills, and processes would interest you?

- How can you vary your routines?

- Who could provide a bridge for you to a different way of seeing or doing something?

If you feel as though you have no discretionary time for yourself, get assistance from one or two creative sources without a vested interest in the outcome. Ask them to help you let go of what you may consider your non-negotiable responsibilities. There has to be at least one that can be postponed, dropped, or delegated, at least for a while.

You'll no doubt notice that the common theme among all these suggestions is becoming more flexible. Go beyond what you know, what's comfortable, what's predictable.

© *Photograph by Zeke Mekonnen*

*Where do you want to cross over? Learning about the history of building any bridge will amaze you, providing many other metaphors related to the struggles to make better connections.*

# Enter Your Zone of Discomfort, Fear, or Anxiety

Whatever makes you feel uncomfortable, fearful, or anxious is likely a good cue to where to take a step. In fact, if you don't feel some sense of discomfort about doing something new, perhaps it's not a worthwhile use of your time. As Debra Winger said at mid-life when she was returning to acting in a new, challenging part,

225

her motivation was simple: "It scared me." In fact, Winger called fear "her useful muse."

For you, what prompts discomfort, fear, or anxiety? Among the many shifts likely to come with a dynamic, rich life that offers opportunities as well as losses, this may include:

- public speaking

- starting a challenging project or connecting with new people

- addressing conflict

- requesting assistance with something that's important to you

- interviewing for different or new work

- entering a different role related to marriage, divorce, home ownership, driving, retirement, parenting, work, finance, achievement, schooling, health, community, or _____.

- losing a cherished person or connection

In any of these or other situations that come to mind, make one choice for action you can responsibly take. What can you say to yourself for encouragement to move forward as you explore the following questions?

- When will you enter your zone of discomfort?

- Who can help you take one step forward?

- How can you prepare and practice before you act?

As you've no doubt discovered already, often the negative fantasies around what will happen are much worse than the actual experience.

Now, allow yourself to proceed. Actually go *through* whatever discomfort, fear, anxiety, or even suffering is entailed in taking wholehearted, responsible action. I bet you'll feel some exhilaration or at least the lightness of relief from your effort. And if not, at minimum you will come closer to moving forward — especially as you follow up with other actions.

## Life-Long Strategies

Throughout the life span, and especially as you mature, there are proven strategies for stretching, strengthening, and enriching your capacities. Here are three that also foster good mental health and a fulfilling life.

***Learning Continuously:*** This can include formal programs and informal projects, as well as modest professional and personal efforts. Reading, conversing, thinking, playing sports, and writing, especially in longhand believe it or not, contribute. So does being involved in one or more of the arts. Among many options, the latter may include crafts, dance, music, photography, art, and design.

***Whether you enjoy getting lost in library stacks, clicking away in e-books and the Internet, exploring new articles and magazines, or listening to and learning from others, snoop regularly. Enrich your mind and possibilities with new, different information.***

***Staying socially involved***: Consider your connections with individuals, groups, and organizations.

- How can you improve their quality, depth, and range?
- How representative are they of your interests and values?
- What one new link will you make this month?

- Which connections will you let go?
- How can you cultivate conversational ease?

© *Photograph by Andrew Winter*

### *Even casual conversations in public areas can open new adventures and vistas or just use time well.*

*Accepting and dealing with ambiguity*: How apt in today's world. You can feel both attracted to and anxious about the unknown, for example. One challenge and opportunity is to create and enjoy as secure an environment as possible, while being alert and preparing for the unexpected. That's one rationale for the lists in Step One.

For example, look at the photograph on the next page to imagine what the images could be and how ambiguity also applies to your life.

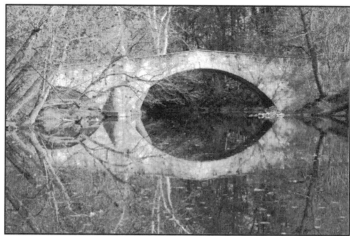

© *Photograph by Andrew Winter*

### *What do you see here?*

Speaking of resilience, neurologist Oliver Sacks says flexibility is crucial. He also lauds the importance of external resources, especially community and family. Ultimately, life-long strategies for effective development and meaning will integrate learning, flexibility, and relationships. The capacity for enhancing all three lies within you.

## The Stories of Your Journeys

As you can imagine, figuring out and appreciating yourself while acting on your goals is a life-long process. Substantial progress does not usually flow easily or logically. At times you may fly around in circles before reaching a more comfortable perch. Periods of calm occur too.

Along the way, perceptions of yourself and the environment will change. Some limitations can be tamed. New doors, or at least windows, may open, bringing variety and vitality to everyday situations. Although incremental work on expressing your courage will never end, results will contribute to self-respect and satisfaction. What better way to use your most precious commodity, time?

How many hours a week will you invest in moving forward, in developing your capacity for courage? Will you at least start to honor your powers and potential with one to two hours?

Use the time to invest in yourself and assist others. Choose and use the keys to becoming courageous in order to discover and express all of your other unique powers — and develop the life you want.

Following is a guide that will help you hear your courage in whatever short story you want to tell about yourself. That process will prove you are already courageous and show you how to hear it in the future.

As with *Choose Courage* in general, please adapt the process to your needs, taking what's useful and leaving the rest. Continue to use your own good resources, judgment, and insight.

# Uncovering Your Courage Through Your Stories

*"Without courage, all other virtues lose their meaning."*
British Prime Minister, Winston Churchill

**PREPARATION**
Under an hour to read, consider and hear your courage in your story

**RESULTS**
- Increased appreciation of yourself and others
- Information and inspiration for continuing action
- Excitement and energy about your possibilities
- Courage to develop your other strengths

- Experience in identifying and promoting your courage

Many people talk about courage, but how can *you* get it? Right now, because you'll learn how to find it within yourself!

This guide provides a process for recognizing your own courage. It also gives you experience and tools for continuing growth. By all means, use it to assist others in accessing their courage.

Just as recognizing your courage will start with your own story, so does this guide. You'll start to hear the themes of courage in even my following brief story.

> *Hunting for a dissertation topic, I had to admit I had breached the line separating exploration from procrastination. But in trying to bring my almost ten-year-old doctoral program to a close, at least I had chosen criteria for a topic. I wanted to work on something interesting enough to keep me going and useful enough to contribute to peoples' lives. Generally I felt uninspired by the narrow, manageable topics so many university advisors and students prefer.*

> *Although I realized I was setting my standards high, I was also being practical. Without an idea that could bring benefits to others and excite me, I was pretty sure I wouldn't finish the tough slog of research, writing, and evaluations by university professors and committees.*

> *The idea for my topic came from a surprising source — while I participated in an informal discussion group related to organizational and management effectiveness. I had decided to attend out of curiosity, not as a degree requirement. During the conventional discussion, a question*

*popped into my mind. "If we know the techniques and how to improve the effectiveness of individuals and organizations, why don't we do it?" Laziness, sabotage, and time constraints didn't seem adequate explanations.*

*I remember feeling excited. All of a sudden I saw a vision — hardly the usual dissertation inspiration. It was a movie marquee surrounded by pulsing yellow klieg lights. Written in bold red letters on the white background was the word COURAGE.*

*I felt impelled to speak. Without knowing what I was going to say, I stood up and started talking. Although I don't recall my exact words, I remember mentioning reasons people don't take effective action even when they know the responsible or appropriate course. Techniques and tools are available. Goals are even defined. Leaders exist. But nothing much happens except talk. Maybe many lack courage!*

*Then I sat down and whispered to the professor next to me: "That's what I want to write about: courage." The idea felt so right — inspiring and useful.*

*Little did I know what lay ahead:*

*Losing trust in and asking that very professor to leave my dissertation committee after he kept repeating the same thoughts at every meeting, as if we had made no progress, and published an article on courage (Anger and frustration were good goads for my action!)*

*Learning and using a new computer system and software at the university after mine crashed*

*Hitting walls on many occasions when I did not know what to do next nor how to interpret information from the research*

*Being left to my own devices by the dissertation committee when they did not understand what I proposed to do (I thought I did, but really didn't. At least they had confidence I could proceed.)*

*Sometimes I felt lost and inadequate, not to mention presumptuous. Studying what others had to say about courage, from the Greeks to modern-day writers, I wondered what I could possibly add. Yet as I kept at it I did not find anyone who described in detail how you and I can become courageous.*

### *End of My Story*

Moralists saw courage as an innate characteristic of particular individuals. Historians wrote about specific deeds that showed it. Neither approach teaches individuals how to develop their own capacity for courage.

If it's an innate characteristic, you either have it or you don't. Case closed. If it's an isolated act, like the Cheshire Cat, it disappears in time with only the smile to remind of what happened. With this interpretation, you're only as courageous as your last act. And if it's merely a set of rational criteria for judgment — you are courageous if — does that tell *you* how to develop your own capacity for courage?

So then I asked myself what point of view might help individuals uncover their capacity for courage? My research in psychology, philosophy, and with individuals led me to see courage as a process of becoming; it was filled with the false starts, regressions, and stasis that mark many efforts to accomplish something of value.

I'll remind you of the definition of this process and some other guidelines from my dissertation later. And don't peek! If you do, you'll rob yourself of the opportunity to appreciate your capacity for courage through your own story.

Right now, all you need to do is tell yourself one story of how you worked through a difficult or challenging situation at the level of detail and approximate length I used in my own story above. Whether dramatic or not, choose one in which your accomplishments or progress, modest or more significant, made *you* feel proud. Include facts, processes and, emotions.

**Stop reading now and let your story flow out, without editing, either by writing or recording it. Then return to this point.**

*©Art by Ani Bustamante*

## *Your stories may be scribbled at first, even nonlinear, but you'll see symbolic themes and overlays.*

Now that you have your story in hand, identify themes related to the facts, emotions and processes. If you have trouble finding the themes, which involves some analysis and synthesis, ask someone to help you name them. In addition, you may see the example of themes I pulled out of my own story in the extended box at the end of this guide. If you don't agree with all of these interpretations, that's all right. Meanings can vary, depending on the source and who's observing the outcome.

Keep your own story in mind as you read the definition and other information related to the generic process of uncovering your courage below. When you are finished reading these descriptions of the process, return to your story again. Use the definitions for finding new examples of your courage that may not have been apparent during your first search for story themes.

**Courage** is a process of becoming that involves:

- the willingness to realize your true capacities

- by going *through* discomfort, fear, anxiety, or suffering

- and taking wholehearted, responsible action

(Notice emotional, intellectual, ethical and spiritual aspects, mentioned in greater detail in Step Five.)

**Willingness** is the process of choosing unconditionally, voluntarily sacrificing alternatives.

**Realize** is to comprehend fully or correctly, to actualize or achieve.

**True** is consistent with reality, genuine, fundamental.

**Capacity** is the ability to hold, do, receive or absorb; the maximum or optimum amount that can be achieved; the ability to learn or retain knowledge; a faculty or aptitude.

**Wholehearted** is to undertake fully with sincerity, openness to experience, compassion, and energy. It is something done for itself, not as a means to an end.

**Responsible** is being ethically accountable, accepting authorship.

**Action** is the process of doing, the transmission of energy, force or influence as the result of responsible thought and intuition.

**Discomfort** is mental or bodily distress.

**Anxiety** is the state of unease and distress about future uncertainties, lacking an unambiguous cause or specific threat.

**Fear** is the feeling of alarm or disquiet caused by the expectation of specific danger, pain or disaster.

**Suffering** is the feeling of actual pain or distress, sustaining of loss, injury, harm, or punishment; the enduring of evil, injury, pain, or death.

# Four Concepts Complementary to Courage

**Authenticity** is the process of realizing your genuine self through openness to yourself and others and receptivity to what you and others offer.

**Commitment** is the process of entrusting yourself to another person, idea, thing, or situation.

**Passion** is the range of emotions and desires, involving pain and pleasure, that focuses your energy for self-enactment.

**Vocation** is the idea or inspiration that gives meaning to your work. It is the calling that enables you to express who you are to yourself and others by producing something you value that also connects to a transcendent purpose.

Even if your story lacks clear examples of the process of finding your courage, it likely has inklings of the capacity within you. Remember that developing it further can be straightforward, nonlinear, a mosaic, or a mix. Looking for neatness could obstruct useful insights about your potential and how to uncover it. And expecting some kind of final, dramatic outcome does damage to seeing your capacity as a process of becoming.

Now that you have a sense of what the process involves, you may want to find a situation to apply what you've learned about your capacity for courage. Consider the following, for example:

- What matter feels manageable, but important enough to you to express your courage now?

- Imagine how you would start taking action. To focus your commitment, say one brief matter out loud that you truly want to do, as clearly and specifically as possible.

- What first step will you take within the next 24 hours?

As you begin, you may see your courage emerge full-blown, as subtle hints of possibilities to come, or somewhere in this continuum. At least, you've started opening yourself to something worth your precious time and energy.

Notice how most steps you take encourage you to move forward again, if only because you've *done something*. Even the mistakes or detours, when you learn from them, are useful. As you continue to realize and express your true capacities, accept the messiness and ambiguity that's appropriate. Enjoy exploring possibilities and celebrating even modest progress. With whom will you like to do that? Finally, ask yourself how you can encourage others to take action too, possibly finding ways to collaborate.

# Finding the themes of courage in Ruth Schimel's dissertation story

| Story | Theme Analysis |
|---|---|
| Hunting for a dissertation topic in the late 1980s, I had to admit that I had breached the line separating exploration from procrastination. | Recognizing and being honest about an internal struggle |
| But in trying to bring my almost ten-year-old doctoral program to a close, at least I had chosen criteria for the topic. I wanted to work on something engaging enough to keep me going and useful enough to contribute to peoples' lives. Generally, I felt uninspired by the narrow manageable topics so many university advisors and students prefer. | Expressing what's truly important |
| Although I realized I was setting my standards high, I was also being practical. Without an idea that could bring benefits to others and excite me, I was pretty sure that I wouldn't finish the tough slog of researching, writing, and evaluations by university professors and committees. | Being clear about what will actually lead to action |

| Story (Continued) | Theme Analysis (Continued) |
|---|---|
| The idea for my topic came from a surprising source —while I participated in an informal discussion related to organizational and management effectiveness. I had decided to attend out curiosity, not as a degree requirement | Doing something for its intrinsic appeal |
| During the conventional discussion, a question popped into my mind. "If we know the techniques and how to improve the effectiveness of individuals and organizations, why don't we do it?" Laziness, sabotage, and time constraints didn't seem adequate explanations. | Asking critical, independent-minded questions, using critical thinking |
| I remember feeling excited. | Being alert to important emotions that indicate preferences |
| All of a sudden I saw a vision — hardly the usual dissertation inspiration. It was a movie marquee surrounded by pulsing yellow klieg lights. Written in bold red letters on the white background was the word **COURAGE.** | Staying open to non-traditional inspiration, visual data, and information |

| **Story (Continued)** | **Theme Analysis (Continued)** |
|---|---|
| I felt impelled to speak. Without knowing what I was going to say, I started talking. Although I don't recall my exact words, I remember mentioning the reasons people don't take effective action even when they know the responsible or appropriate course. Techniques and tools are available. Goals are even defined. Leaders exist. But nothing much happens except talk. Maybe many lack courage! | Saying what is believed without editing, speaking from the heart |
| Then I sat down and whispered to the professor next to me, "That's what I want to write about: Courage." The idea felt so right, inspiring, and useful. | Committing to an authentic goal |
| Little did I know what lay ahead:<br>• Losing trust in and asking that very professor to leave my dissertation committee after he kept repeating the same thoughts at every meeting, as if we had made no progress, and published an article on courage. | Doing uncomfortable and perhaps risky, but necessary, things; converting anger or frustration to positive action |
| • Learning and using a new computer system and software at the university after mine crashed | Persisting through difficulties and ignorance; learning new things |

| Story (Continued) | Theme Analysis (Continued) |
|---|---|
| • Hitting walls on many occasions when I did not know what to do next nor how to interpret information from the research | Persisting through difficulties and ignorance; learning new things |
| • Being left to my own devices by the dissertation committee when they did not understand what I proposed to do. They thought I understood, though I really didn't. At least, they had confidence that I could proceed. | Continuing to persist despite a void in understanding and assistance |
| Sometimes I felt lost and inadequate, not to mention presumptuous. | Admitting anxiety and naming it clearly |
| Studying what others had to say about courage, from the Greeks to modern day writers, I wondered what I could possibly add. Yet as I kept at it I did not find anyone who described in detail **how** you and I can become courageous. | Following through to meet a significant, worthwhile goal, despite doubts |

# STEP SIX:
# Taking Action

## You have the power.

*"Whatever course you decide upon, there is always someone to tell you that you are wrong. There are always difficulties arising which tempt you to believe that your critics are right. To map out a course of action and follow it to an end requires courage. "*
American essayist, lecturer and poet, Ralph Waldo Emerson

*If you want to identify me, ask me not where I live or want to eat, or how I comb my hair, but ask me what I am living for, in detail, and ask me what I think is keeping me from living fully for the thing I want to live for.*
Trappist monk and writer, Thomas Merton

*Courage is the process of becoming willing to realize your true capacities by going* **through** *discomfort, fear, anxiety, or suffering and taking wholehearted, responsible action.*
Definition of the process of becoming courageous from Ruth Schimel's dissertation research with everyday people

In Step Five you saw how just one of your own stories could prove you're already courageous. Of course other people's experiences can provide models, inspiration, and entertainment. But relying on them primarily for motivation and guidance may distract as you pursue your unique needs and interests.

Why? Comparisons may make you feel less capable. They could distort the work and enjoyment of investing in your own development.

Comparisons are also specious; you are not the other person, nor do you share their situation and background. Instead, move from observing others' experiences to being the author of your own life, from thinking and talking to action. Appreciating what you can do and following through with authentic choices will probably be more satisfying anyway

Your strengths and interests are a fruitful, accessible garden for planting the seeds of courage. As they grow, you'll be honoring your past and nurturing your potential for being more fully realized. With even modest actions, you'll see how the process of becoming courageous offered in this book is within your grasp now.

At the same time, feel free to adapt and transplant relevant ideas from others' stories to your own turf when it's useful. If you wish, practice doing that when you watch an illustrated talk about adventure photography and personal transformation.

Just remember, do not compare yourself to Michael. It's his 16-minute story at the link, not yours. Instead, consider which aspects can be used in your situation. For example, they may include how he worked through fears, benefitted from support, and courted luck. http://tedxtalks.ted.com/video/TEDxBG-Michael-Brown-How-Storie

Now, back to harvesting your own stories for direction and guidance. In addition to reminders of your strengths, progress, and accomplishments, they:

- could remind you of valuable, previous approaches and actions that can be brought forward

- are easier to remember than dry facts and linear, logical ideas

- capture the essence of experiences that can't be measured or narrowed into neat categories

- provide hope, inspiration, and other encouragement about what currently appears ordinary or problematic in your life

- contain subtle leads, clues, and visions not available in others' stories

When you take a little time to unpack some of your stories related to difficult or challenging situations, be alert for the possibilities suggested in the bullets above and others below. Though aspects may be low-key, you'll probably find more novelty and drama, not to mention courage, than you expect. (For your own story analysis, see Step Five, How to Start, and the guide at the end: *Uncovering Your Courage through Your Stories*.)

To continue mining your experience, imagine a few stories in the movie of your mind. As possible instances, choose one or two from the following that you want to remember.

When you:

- were moved deeply or felt good about something that you did and wanted to repeat

- expressed specifically what you felt to someone you cherish

- used your true capacities, however you defined them at the time (or use these possible criteria: time went very quickly, what you did had meaning to you, and you couldn't wait to do what you were doing)

- felt honored by notice of an accomplishment you also valued

- worked through something difficult, intimidating, frustrating, or scary that was truly important to you

- wrote or spoke effectively about something important to you

- said *no* productively, comfortably, and graciously

- said *yes* in spite of discomfort, anxiety, fear, or another inhibiting emotion

- were explicit with others about what you wanted

Appreciate and jot down a few of the main themes of your related courageous actions, from modest to significant, that come to mind. If nothing emerges, maybe the following points, singly or together will remind you of stories you want to tell. They may also help you find catalysts in current situations, what could have meaning and motivation for you now. What one or two ring your bells of memory?

- romance or ardent emotional attachment related to people, ideas, visions, or dreams

- power issues in families, groups, tribes, organizations, communities, nations, and elsewhere

- comedy, absurdity, and humor from puns to belly laughs

- tragedy ranging from deep disappointment to significant loss

- mystery or just suspense about "what next?"

- ghosts or hangovers of previous experiences or issues

- seemingly magical or useful coincidences that can come when you've proceeded with any combination of curiosity, vision, and commitment

- conflict: perceived or actual, confining or creative, destructive or productive

- adventure and exploration, conventional or not

Do you notice any common themes beneath the obvious plots of stories that come to mind now? For example, one might be what happened when you dropped social acts, props, labels, facades, snits, masks, and other ways your true self is obscured and range limited. Removing such energy suckers and distractions can open yourself to others — and yourself.

As actress, country singer, mother, wife, and foodie Gwyneth Paltrow said:

> *"I'm good at acting, but I may be more inclined to do something that I'm less good at and more interested in. The most dangerous thing is buying into an idea of what you're supposed to be, the projection of what people think you are. If I've done the best I can do and my intentions are super clear, then it's really not my business what anybody thinks of me."*

Whether or not you have any of Paltrow's interests or capacities, you still have the choice of removing cloaks or disguises you've donned or others impose. Imagine what would happen when you allow your true nature to come through even an interesting jungle of distractions. Consider film director Sidney Lumet's reminder: "All good work is self-revelation."

249

© *Art by Ani Bustamante*

However modest your choices and actions, any one of them can spark other abilities, prompting unexpected benefits. Each could confirm or reveal purposes that have significance for you. Use this Step Six to guide you through creating cycles of empowering action for realizing your true capacities. You'll see how to bring together ideas, processes, and actions for focus to support your progress.

To remind of the resources in *Choose Courage*, here is a brief summary of the Steps in this book.

- **Step One** prepares you for action, answering why you should bother to access your capacity for courage. It also shows how a specific array of often messy and uncontrollable influences makes life naturally complex. In spite of these realities, situations where you do have influence and choices are offered.

- **Step Two** helps you get ready to realize your courage: being authentic, entrusting yourself to someone or something beyond you through commitment, appreciating the emotions that energize your passions, and expressing yourself through creating what you value or vocation.

- **Steps Three and Four** show how to identify barriers of negative thinking and emotions as well as experiences that may be holding you back. They provide ways to transcend them, freeing energy and hope for action.

- **Step Five** describes the new meaning of courage from original research, how it emerges and what you can do to make it work for you. It also shows you how to use your own stories to prove your courage as catalyst and inspiration to move forward.

- **Step Six** now supports your continuing voyage of choosing courage through strengthening cycles of action and accomplishments.

© *Photograph by Andrew Winter*

### *Will you be stuck in a narrow passage with limited light or move through it?*

## Attend and be kind to yourself while addressing realities.

As you adapt and apply the guidance and suggestions from *Choose Courage* and make progress using other sources as well, rest along the way. More activity is not always better.

Since time out is important in the process of becoming courageous, find places to park. In any peaceful place, breathe deeply, quiet your mind and meditate in whatever forms work for you, as regularly as possible. If you don't already do this, perhaps explore:

- Diaphragmatic Breathing:
  en.wikipedia.org/wiki/Diaphragmatic_breathing

- Meditation: en.wikipedia.org/wiki/Meditation;

252

- The Incredible Power of Concentration: www.flixxy.com/the-incredible-power-of-concentration-miyoko-shida.htm#.UY4ZgYWbKME

Whether you use such processes or others, sustain rhythms that work for you, including listening to your intuition, letting things percolate, and taking small steps that have meaning for you.

© *Photograph by Amé Solomon*

### *Meeting nature half way...*

Another choice to weave into your rhythms, if not already part of them, is Jonah Lehrer's advice in his Wall Street Journal article, *Mom Was Right: Go Outside*. "After a brief exposure to the outdoors, people are more creative, happier, and better able to focus. If there were a pill that delivered these same results, we'd all be popping it."

Your brief and longer stops to relax and refresh are crucial for renewing yourself and allowing ideas and opportunities to evolve. Like a satisfying soup, flavors, and nutrition meld with time and periodic, gentle stirring.

As you experiment with better ways to be present on a reasonably rhythmic basis, vary your activities; for ideas, explore the choices for pampering yourself in Step Two.

Even small amounts of such renewal will provide perspective, likely mitigating the natural discomfort and instability that come with everyday life. Any respite can range from minutes to hours to days to weeks or more. Insofar as possible, modify your patterns to see what works to promote ease and support your progress. Perhaps share routines of rest with people you like or cherish.

As you know already, emotions can thwart as well as empower action. Both rational and non-rational goals ebb and flow as reality intrudes. So many choices and mixed motivations cloud decisions.

And as you've experienced, changes outside and within yourself bring new challenges and opportunities. Like the process of choosing courage, much of life is nonlinear and fluid. Although calling sections of this book Steps may imply progress proceeds along a clear path, the design and content reflects a far less neat reality. They invite you to engage at any point that has some promise of being useful and inspiring. Throughout, test choices for assistance, open new doors, and ride the waves, staying alert to being true to yourself.

***Waves of living may move from rough and threatening to buoyant calm.***

# Ways to find right proportion and comfort while sustaining focus

Maybe the following themes will be useful by providing structure and stability, especially during often wavy transitions. By all means adjust interpretations and actions to what works well for you.

### Your center, your core for action:

The design of *Choose Courage* honors your nature and wish to continue creating what you truly want. Starting within yourself first will help you avoid the ping pong of maybe this, maybe that when you react to externals first.

Using the tools and inspiration, you'll continue to uncover your unique and valuable self. That includes your values, skills, passions, and interests. As they are reflected in your actions, satisfying outcomes will add hope to the mix. Even some rowdy genetic predispositions and psychological imprints can be harnessed into productive behavior when you understand them and are ready to ride. Will you have a new description of a skill: the self-whisperer?

## *Your thoughts and emotions:*

Challenge them when they are negative, determining if they're true or accurate. If you're not sure, test them against reality and with others you trust. Consider what you can learn from them. In any event, keep working on how to avoid repetition that has not helped you. Decide whether or not you'll succumb to unproductive patterns yet again, getting assistance in moving forward as need be.

When positive and encouraging, use such emotions as catalysts for action now. Their energy will contribute to better results and be useful to call up for future reference. Together, healthy thinking and emotions will help you go through challenging times — and enjoy the present.

## *Your bonds:*

Based on experience, you can probably expect relationships and your environment to be in various states of flux. People rarely want the same things at the same time in the same way. Situations change around you. To provide anchors, cultivate worthwhile connections based on trust, honesty, patience, and reciprocity.

Since you're unlikely to progress significantly without some support, seek and cherish the good connections that have meaning for you. Consider letting go of relationships based on habit alone, especially when the flow is one way. You'll probably know it's time to do so when you regularly seek ways to avoid or feel tired after being with a person or group.

In contrast, the healthy relationships you have and develop will provide satisfaction and meaning as well as chances for mutual assistance. To ensure their quality, take the risks of gentle frankness that are needed, celebrate their value together, and do the work they deserve. Find ways to include fun along the way.

© *Photograph by Andrew Winter*

### *Conversation and conviviality with people you care about bring pleasure and delight.*

## *Your opportunities in challenges:*

The very situations that seem to thwart you such as difficulties, messes, and discomfort can be signals for self-discovery and growth. As you work through them, they can convert to adventures and new creativity. You'll be building your courage muscles.

To prepare for action, attend to what's unfolding and what could happen; design simple, viable plans when appropriate while being spontaneous and intuitive. Find partners to practice and produce. As a Peace Corps volunteer once said, "When things are hard, they're good."

## *Your efficiency:*

Repetition of behavior based on fear or anxiety and negative thinking may provide the empty, transitory comfort of predictability. It can also waste time by providing escapes from positive action. Worse, the automatic responses embedded in them often thwart worthwhile outcomes and discourage others from providing assistance because they cannot see your healthier motivation. Instead of letting unproductive habits gobble precious time and limit possibilities, wrangle them into submission or store them for later investigation.

## *Your powers:*

As you continue to strengthen and expand your capacities, you'll increase your influence over your life, but never be in total control. Your power lies in the choices you develop and use, how you clarify priorities and take action. That will likely lead to serving your needs and dreams as well as contributing to others. You'll also find the array of riches and delightful surprises life offers more accessible. Table 6.1 on the following page shows opportunities for effective action during natural transitions.

*Table 6.1*

## OPPORTUNITIES FOR EFFECTIVE ACTION DURING NATURAL TRANSITIONS

- Seek ways to improve clarity, depth, and growth in your core characteristics.

- Test negative thoughts and emotions against reality and with others; write down positive ones for encouragement, review, and reflection over time.

- Cherish and cultivate good connections.

- Use challenges as catalysts in self-discovery and development.

- Save time and energy by avoiding repetition of unproductive or destructive patterns.

- Stay alert to what's unfolding in order to prepare and plan.

- Create meaning from the inside out by basing authentic choices and actions on your values and principles.

- Mine and express the strengths within you first.

- Find support and patience to promote progress.

- Consider and adapt others' advice, but don't gobble it whole; use critical thinking.

## *Your deeper sources:*

Dig below the surface, working from the inside out. Let the choices you make and actions you take reflect your values and principles, your spirit, as much as possible. That will likely bring inspiration as well as calm and focus based on what's truly important to you.

Though there can be leaps forward, generally progress is incremental. Causal relationships between what you do and results are rarely neat. Occasionally, loops and regression occur.

The continuing process requires irretrievable time so use it as well as you can. In this crucible of development, others' faith and support, coupled with your own concrete, healthy actions, are crucial. Given the derivation of the word patience, as with passion, some suffering could be involved. Just make sure it's worthwhile rather than masochistic, that you learn from it.

## *Others' advice:*

No guidance — even from this book — when you use it, is likely to work well unless you adapt it authentically and do due diligence to test its relevance. However well-meaning the advice, be alert to how it may mirror the experience and needs of friends, colleagues, mentors, and family rather than reflect what's appropriate for you.

# Bottom line?

So many immediately accessible as well as latent riches are within you. Adapt and use the guidance and suggestions throughout *Choose Courage* to mine your possibilities and express your powers.

At the same time, the growth process might expose your own ambivalence about being powerful. To transcend such inhibitions, take regular, small steps, while exploring how well founded your concerns are about flexing your muscles. Use your imagination and creativity; ask what's the worst thing that could happen and figure out how you'd handle that. Continue to employ good judgment, especially as you learn from people in your corner who appreciate your true self.

Keep activating and enjoying applying the following capacities on your own and with guidance from *Choose Courage* and other sources:

- skills and abilities

- interests and passions

- values and principles

- intuition and instincts

Confidence strengthens how you express what makes you who you are. In turn, the moderate and major transitions that make life naturally challenging are there to influence rather than intimidate.

Part of the foundation of this book, designed to support your intrinsic courage and capacity for growth, are two basic related ideas: the value of process and the philosophy of existentialism. As you've already seen explicitly and implicitly, the very nature of becoming courageous is a process. Investing in *how* you do something, as well as what you do, will help you meet your goals more effectively.

## The power of process today

During a Thanksgiving dinner, I watched two brothers, eight and ten, immersed in competing with one another in several games. Most of their play time went to showing off their cleverness to one another and the observing adults. Each seemed harnessed to getting it over on the other. The actual wins occurred in several seconds. Then what? Another game, another deal, another race?

© *Photograph by Andrew Winter*

### *Once the seduction of speed or focus on winning alone takes over, what's next?*

Impatient to finish each game, the boys reminded me of many adults. They focused on the ends, ignoring the pleasure and possibilities of the means or process where most time and effort typically goes. Though likely uninteresting to them, alternatives to their win-lose approach might have included:

- making up a game with different outcomes such as win-win

- creating and expressing their own fantasies rather than following someone else's rules

- having fun being silly, sometimes a prelude to creativity and dropping traditional, established or rigid roles

- including others in the process for variety and fun

262

- learning why they are engaged and how that could transfer to another activity

In addition to their competitive habits, maybe the boys were also conditioned by the speed of smart phones, video games, computers, constant contact of social media, and remote controls. Together, the technology tends to accustom many people to quick fixes, limited communication, reactive behavior, and instant gratification.

As with the boys, such experiences put focus on the recipient, as well as outcomes rather than being in the moment. The "big bang" of an immediate win becomes more important than playing itself.

And so go many activities in professional and personal life, symbolically and actually. The subtle pleasures and possibilities of process get lost in the immediacy of outputs, including clicks, texts, buzzes, e-mails, and screen swipes.

When do such reactions just become conditioned or automatic and when are they consciously chosen and used well? How is the quality of life affected by their ubiquity, especially over time?

## The idea of process from past to present

Though facts and information are more likely to be taught and respected in Western culture, attention to process certainly is not new. Early Greek philosophers such as Parmenides, Zeno, and the Pre-Socratic Atomists recognized its essential value. They believed that natural existence consists in and is best understood in terms of *processes* rather than *things*. Reality is movement, not stasis.

Relatively recent insights reflected this perspective as well. Starting in the 1800s, confirmations existed in geology (Lyall) and logic (Hegel). Today, much of the focus of natural and social science practice has shifted focus from products or things to developmental, process-oriented views.

Think of this natural fluidity as a constant as you make choices and take action. In *The Evolving Self*, Harvard developmental psychologist Robert Kegan compares the person "as much to an activity as to a thing — an ever progressive motion engaged in giving itself a new form."34 He notes Western culture still has residue of an absolute distinction between things or entities and processes or activities.

## Assumptions about objectivity

You'll hear this residue in the belief that there can be an entirely objective view, that omniscience is possible. Anything else is subjective and therefore less trustworthy or true. Yet neither perspective exists in pure or exact form because each actor or observer will filter perceptions based on experience, education, and emotion, to name just some influences. Regardless of scientific controls and checks or other ways to ensure replicable outcomes unconscious bias cannot be avoided.

A history of science such as Thomas Kuhn's *The Nature of Scientific Revolutions* describes how what is considered objective or true just reflects the current belief system, often supported by the current establishment. Only when enough exceptions accumulate does new information put previous "evidence and facts" in question.

Practitioners of the social *sciences* perhaps took on the label of science to enhance their credibility. But even in the often more mathematically-based economics, many hedged their bets with two main assumptions. Ironically, both could preclude data related to real life: ceteris paribus (other things being equal or held constant) and rational man. Each is unlikely given the dynamism of life and the complex motivations and behavior of human beings.

Thank goodness, the naïve assumption that man (or woman) is rational is now being enriched and updated by the recent infusion of psychology into economics. But it started a while back in 1976 with Tibor Scitovsky's *The Joyless Economy: The Psychology of Human Satisfaction.* As with other interdisciplinary approaches in all the sciences, behavioral economics recognizes the complexity of human motivation, nature, and interaction among many variables.

In contrast, much thinking and observation in Eastern and other cultures can be more open. For example, the Chinese do not tend to splice reality into either/or, black and white.

Attention to the reality and value of process finesses such dichotomies and the illusion of objectivity. What's left then? Instead of seeing objectivity and subjectivity as incompatible, find the overlaps, where understanding, useful action, good communication, and ethical concerns meet in real life. Such an approach is called intersubjectivity, suggested by Berger and Luckmann in their *Social Construction of Reality.*

## Process underlies action, conscious and unconscious

Being alert to process, or how something unfolds, offers such possibilities for finding common ground and useful understanding about human prospects and action. Going a little deeper into what it involves promises benefits. Kegan mentions philosopher Alfred North Whitehead's view of life as motion itself versus just a thing in motion.

This perspective comes fully alive as you consider how your body works, the brain in particular. Through the 100 trillion or so spaces between neurons, called synapses, information from your conscious and unconscious choices is transmitted via electro-chemical processes. In response, the full body adjusts, responds, renews, and initiates.

Since skin is permeable, the electrical impulses of the entire nervous system could possibly extend beyond the body. If you want to see a resulting aura of light, explore Kirlian photography. http://en.wikipedia.org/wiki/Kirlian_photography

Anticipating the dynamism of the atom, Whitehead said:

> *"The principle of process is stated in this way: That **how** an actual entity becomes constitutes what that actual entity is; so that the two descriptions of an actual entity are not independent. It's 'being' is constituted by its 'becoming'."*[35]

If this language seems somewhat stiff, appreciate its soul by remembering how a child develops. Already affected by hormonal, environmental, and other influences through the umbilical cord as well as genetic predispositions, a baby is in growth mode from its start. Later, the interactions among the child, other people, and the environment all result in a human be*ing*, evolving over time. Even this word for a person is an action verb.

## Emotion and rationality

Defining courage as a process of becoming in this book honors this dynamism of your life. To remind, the process involves being willing to realize your true capacities by going through discomfort, fear, anxiety, or suffering and taking wholehearted, responsible action. Cross the bridge to your courage by going *through* challenging emotions and situations. Steps Three and Four are designed to help you "get over it."

As you've probably found, the bridge can be blocked, not only by your own habits, but also by attitudes and actions of others. Think about how emotion is disdained or avoided by many in Western cultures. Considered a saboteur of rationality, emotion is often equated with subjective bias, diminished capacity, or even loss of control. In contrast, the use of reason is seen as a source and test of knowledge.[36] Yet, as discussed in Steps Three and Four, emotion is not only necessary for rationality or reason, but also brings energy and meaning, allies in authentic action.

In sum, I think pure reason and total objectivity are likely illusions anyway. As my engineer father explained to me, what may seem a blue sky is actually gray; it just seems blue due to the refraction of light on the dust particles in the air. Regarding other sense-based perceptions, recent studies have shown that holding a hot cup of liquid or being in a comfortable chair or environment changes people's behavior.[37] Exposures to various colors also are known to change moods.

In fact, one of the foundations for reason is knowledge which varies with culture and learning, with perceivers and their conscious and unconscious interests. To make sense of such variety and variables, the humanities often open the doors to understanding.

With his quote below, poet William Blake captures the links among reason, knowledge, emotion, ethics, commitment, and other aspects of the process of becoming courageous. In other words, as the old Prego spaghetti sauce ad says, "It's all in there!"

In his introduction to *Songs of Experience*, Blake brings together themes of rational and non-rational forms of knowledge with the process of choosing courage:

> *"Knowledge is not a looseleaf notebook of facts. Above all it is a responsibility for the integrity of what we are, primarily of what we are as ethical creatures. The personal commitment of a man to his skill, the intellectual commitment, and the emotional equipment working together as one, has made the Ascent of Man."*[38]

Until diverse views can be aired, discussed openly, and connections found, ways to bridge such rich complexity for mutual benefit may remain unexplored. Given all the interacting influences affecting individual ways of seeing and interpreting, with ever changing, fluid external situations, it's almost miraculous people find common ground or cause.

Yet making creative connections is certainly possible, especially when people act authentically, from the inside out. Then trust may develop, supporting the risk of openness. In the process, exploration, and productivity may also be expanded.

## How existentialism honors emotion, process, thought, and action

A way of thinking or philosophical movement known as existentialism connects these ideas. In its perspective, making sense of living:

- begins with the individual rather than externals

- assumes a person who thinks, is a center of feeling, initiator of action and

- considers that human existence precedes a separate essence.

Therefore:

- Human nature is not fixed.

- The core of a person consists of freedom, decision and responsibility, or the ability to shape the future through the quest for authentic self-hood.

- The quest is poignant because it can also include a sense of mortality, guilt, alienation, and despair.[39]

These last two bullets offer a way to transcend either/or thinking and acting. Replacing *or* with *and*, one question to explore could be: How can you extract opportunities from difficulties and losses in life while taking action to shape results you value? Or how can you be independent and collaborative?

© *Photograph by Andrew Winter*

## *Where are the connections, support, and cohesiveness for your voyage?*

Even positive experiences can bring challenges and discomfort as routines, identity, and relationships shift. Examples might range from an outstanding personal achievement to a promotion, from a new home to a new love, from mastering new skills to improving appearance and health.

In other words, your willingness to deal with even positive, significant shifts as well as the speed bumps of life sets the stage for choosing courage. Use such challenges to stop and absorb their meaning; take a while longer to think and feel deeply. Those choices will likely provide a sounder basis for effective choice and action.

As you face any barriers that block your wholehearted, responsible action, consider how to make the most of your choices. You can express and combine your authenticity, commitment, passion, or vocation in whatever modest ways that work for you. Perhaps re-visit Step Two to adapt relevant suggestions. Each action confirms you as the agent of your own development. As you take charge, you'll be less likely to ignore or veer away from what your heart and head want.

## Four approaches to encourage yourself and support continuing action in your interest

Political activist Donna Brazile quoted her mother while participating in an academic panel: "It's not what you're called, it's what you answer to." I think action with meaning answers to at least yourself: your values, interests, passions, and use of your capacities by exploring what calls you in work.

Yet you may still wonder about the *why bother* question addressed at the start of *Choose Courage* in Step One. "Bother" only if you want to improve your life and appreciate how to use the true, valuable choices in your hands.

I hope the following four processes and approaches will help you continue your creation of meaning and pleasure for the better life you want. While you cannot force good results, you can promote them. Ultimately choosing courage, as with many valuable possibilities in life, can start gently with a leap of faith. I believe that's a realistic, possible prelude to bringing a concrete range of benefits and delights to life.

# Approach One: Name your motivators, choose your routines

Few of us can echo ambitious efforts similar to "the Bills" — Gates and Clinton — and other leaders who try to promote peace and welfare in the world. In fact as you know, neither man started so grandly initially. To embrace true possibilities through modest efforts, start within your own situation where you have influence and choice. Perhaps these two explorations could help:

- What are the one or two main principles or basic assumptions you believe in? You no doubt can list them off the top of your head right now. For example, I believe most people have the capacity for courage, a great catalyst for their own contributions and development.

- Imagine how you would persist in the face of one crucial setback or challenge you anticipate. To start, this could involve naming a few specific, manageable adjustments in routines that no longer serve you. What small shift in behavior will you make now? For example, I could stop bringing chocolate covered bananas into the house. To prepare more fully, do a short, bulleted outline of how you can and will deal with a specific situation. Keep it to half a page to avoid feeling overwhelmed with to-dos.

# Approach Two: Gentle moves

But you still might prefer the seeming ease and predictability of known routines or just marking time. You may continue to question why you need to take new action at all since fate will pounce and force outcomes beyond your control anyway.

Whether or not this is your point of view, here are some general encouragements and questions, or at least gentle prods, to launch yourself periodically. After skimming them, choose or adapt one you think would work for you.

- No matter what limitations you face, remind yourself that you are capable at least of one useful action now. Name that one you would want to and will do within the next few days. How will you ensure follow through?

- Attend to what's truly important to yourself in any moves you make. Whatever happens, at least ask what you've learned from your choice to act or not to act. How would you apply that learning in the future?

- When hesitating, ask yourself: Would anyone else be able to do what you can do for yourself as well and authentically?

- No matter what your age and situation, how will you use and benefit from the gift of any amount of time available to you today?

- Will you use your mind regularly or let it go fallow? Happily, researchers have found most human brains can regenerate throughout the maturing process. Whether body or mind, what would you really enjoy stretching now? Schedule one action today or tomorrow.

- Situations will shift anyway. Do you want to influence them in your favor or not? If you do, what one action can you take and what resources do you have at hand to use?

# Approach Three: Menu for the whole enchilada

You'll find a range of considerations and activities to guide yourself forward in the following menus of choices. Use them especially if you sense your routines and views of current resources need nutrition. Please consider critically the whole approach in the three boxes below, *Moving through Feeling Fuzzy, Frustrated, or Stuck to Action,* that I developed for my clients.

Change whatever you wish. Add ideas, insights, and information to each list or modify the order within and between the lists. Aspects can relate to your personal as well as professional development. Among the boxes there are many options that interact and support one another.

***Be spicy and healthy in your thinking! Possibly imagine you have the pizzazz or energy of a "red hot chili pepper."***

For any element that relates to your situation, briefly jot down what comes to mind. Start with anything you will do that is possible, likely, or productive. If needed, refer to the examples provided at the end of each box for inspiration, adding whatever sparks of flavor that come to your fertile mind.

# Moving through to action: Present Situation

*Table 6.2*

---

**Present Situation**

(Known to you now)

*Questions:*
- What appeals?
- What dissatisfies?
- What can be improved?
- How?
- What's acceptable?
- What limits you?

*Considerations:*
- Assumptions
- Influences
- Ideas
- Environmental issues
- Internal limitations
- External limitations
- Fears and anxiety

*Capacities & Strengths*
- Skills
- Abilities
- Experience
- Aptitudes
- Knowledge
- Values
- Passions

---

Table 6.2 illustrates the present situation (known to you now). Examples of your possible responses for any you choose are:

*What appeals:* being with people I care about, reading for fun, playing sports, and enjoying work

*What dissatisfies:* avoiding healthy eating and exercise habits; unproductive routines of dealing with bosses and colleagues; acting on impatience, boredom, or fear rather than using good judgment

*What can be improved:* bringing use of time into sync with my top two or three priorities

## Moving through to action: Seeming Muddle in the Middle

Table 6.3 illustrates the muddle in the middle and suggests processes for progress. Here are examples of possible responses to some of the bullets at the top of the column. Use them to launch your own approaches for any one of them.

*Experimenting:* practicing saying *no* when I don't want to or cannot do something

*Discerning:* choosing to be with people who seem worthwhile and trustworthy

*Practicing:* improving my listening skills by asking open-ended questions and acknowledging others' emotions

*Table 6.3*

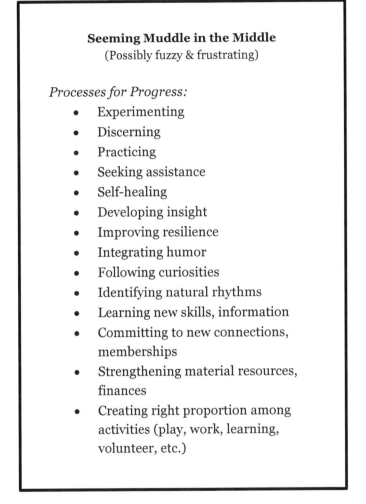

**Seeming Muddle in the Middle**
(Possibly fuzzy & frustrating)

*Processes for Progress:*
- Experimenting
- Discerning
- Practicing
- Seeking assistance
- Self-healing
- Developing insight
- Improving resilience
- Integrating humor
- Following curiosities
- Identifying natural rhythms
- Learning new skills, information
- Committing to new connections, memberships
- Strengthening material resources, finances
- Creating right proportion among activities (play, work, learning, volunteer, etc.)

## Moving through to action: Vision of Your Future (To imagine and investigate)

Table 6.4 illustrates the vision for your future. Think about concrete applications to your situation as you read.

*Table 6.4*

---

**Vision for Your Future**
(To imagine and investigate)

*Integrating insights, emotions, information,
connections, capacities, hopes and
discipline:*

- Expressing to yourself what you
  want to do
- Testing ideas through research,
  conversation
- Refining ideas
- Focusing, planning
- Obtaining, exchanging support,
  resources
- Taking action
- Refining through iterations
- Congratulating and rewarding
  yourself for any progress
- Staying open to new experiences,
  possibilities

---

The following are examples of actions to get you started on moving through the list in Table 6.4:

*Expressing to yourself what you want to do:* saying in my own words what's important to me periodically, reminding myself with calendar prompts

*Testing ideas through research and conversation:* after doing some imaginative snooping, starting an open conversation about what I've learned with someone I respect

*Refining ideas:* developing a simple set of questions to test the viability of what I think I want to do

## Now is the time

Now is the time to think through one lead you've chosen above from your own descriptions of actions you'll take. Use them to start a short, viable plan with bullets taking no more than several lines. When inspired, you can create a more holistic vision, perhaps with a diagram of the flow of action. Since situations, resources, and motivations change, you can update your vision over time. Whatever design you use, possibly address matters such as:

- What: Your manageable goal for the next _____ months?

- How: Specific steps and resources you'll need to get there

- When: timing, including starting dates, interim benchmarks, and completion date

- Who: Names of several people who will assist you and from whom you could learn

- Other considerations you may want to include:

At least dive into any aspect of the menu that strikes your fancy right now rather than putting off action entirely; the longer you postpone something, the less likely you'll do it, I bet. Keep in mind that the process is not entirely linear; the questions, processes, and actions can all interact and strengthen one another.

# Approach Four: Cycles of development

As you use and adapt this approach to action and integrate what you're already doing, you may notice that certain cycles emerge. In my research on how people discover their capacity for courage, three cycles became apparent.

© *Photograph by Andrew Winter*

## *How will you generate your own cycles or symmetries?*

With each one, individuals' emotional, intellectual, spiritual, and ethical muscles seemed to strengthen, making better results more likely. Among the three cycles below, see what seems related to your situation. Follow up with whatever small shifts make sense for your life. Of course, adapt the bullets in the cycles as you wish or create your own cycles based on your insight, instincts, and experience.

# First Cycle

- wanting something very much expressed via a passion or purpose

- being aware of discomfort, anxiety, fear, or guilt

- taking support from others

- believing in concrete, especially beneficial values

- seeing reality

# Second Cycle

- experiencing and naming a range of feelings

- being willing to do work and endure pain, discomfort, or tension appropriate to a situation of value

- making choices, letting go of some possibilities

- taking appropriate, ethical action

- gaining additional insight into and appreciation of your true self though learning, action, and feedback from others

- continuing the dialogue about what's important with yourself and others

- taking good care of yourself

# Third Cycle

- renewing periodically insights about yourself through life experience, dialogue, and contemplation

- integrating true capacities, purpose, passion, and values through action

- enjoying the ongoing creation of meaning in life

- continuing to develop through the cycles and processes mentioned above

# Adapt and follow through on the approaches above

Select and use any previous ideas, information, and suggestions that relate to your situation. Choose among whatever questions below that you know will help you focus and act.

1. What unfinished business would you like to deal with now? What one specific related, manageable action will you take? When?

2. How would you start to describe or clarify a reachable vision or purpose for your life that you'd like to explore and express?

3. What will you do to honor several specific accomplishments, tangible and intangible? They can be modest, conventional, original, significant, or any combination of characteristics that appeal to you.

4. With whom will you share and celebrate your progress?

As always, make whatever changes in the approaches and suggestions you like. Update your ideas and activities at regular intervals that you choose. Create and act on alerts or reminders you create to keep your positive rhythm going.

*Image is in the public domain believed to be free to use without restriction in the US.*

### *What's buzzing in you fertile brain that will lead you forward?*

### *How will you pollinate the worlds within and your reachable goals?*

As I hope I've made clear, choosing courage is a continuing process of becoming. Though there are no quick fixes, there are many ways to step into the life you want, on your own as well as with others you value.

Experiment with ways to honor who you truly are while continuing to grow and learn. Attend to what you see that has value and find ways to uncover what's unseen. Act as if you are in constant emergence, as implied in the metaphors of growth and development in the following poem.

## Springing Forth, Whatever Your Season

by Ruth M. Schimel

*As the gentle spring air unlayers you*
*the clarion yellow of the forsythia*
*calls forth its first leaves.*
*Then the lank willow branches*
*unfurl their veil of peri-dots.*
*No longer snow-blind*
*Your eyes and heart take joy in new bloomings.*
*Or maybe petal deaths make room for new*
*growth,*
*Proving the continuing potential and power of*
*your life.*

# Endings can be beginnings

However uncomfortable the thought of the finality of life, memories of my parents continue to give hope. For example, I smile when I think about my mother's gratitude for her "marbles and mobility," well into her nineties.

I find being aware of my own mortality, which I find more palatable as I make progress with my dreams, is a great motivator for action in the present. That awareness is especially catalytic for significant matters I tend to avoid.

Perhaps keeping in mind this prime epiphany of people at the end of their lives will contribute to your motivation: *I wish I had the courage to live a life true to myself, not the life others expected for me.*

For related rewarding explorations, inspirations, and insights see www.inspirationandchai.com, a blog by an Australian palliative care nurse.

May you continue choosing courage and creating the meaning in life that touches your heart and mind-as well as make a positive difference for others.

# Online Directory of Links and Books

This is an online directory for *Choose Courage: Step into the Life You Want*. Including only a sampling of the wide range of Internet resources you may explore independently, it just summarizes links within this book to assist you on your journey.

Since the Internet is continuously changing, you may not find all the links. When a site has moved you may find a link to a new location. If not, try a search engine such as Google or Bing to find resources and continue learning about subjects of interest.

At the end is a list of relevant books, with emphasis on stories, that may enrich your process of *Choosing Courage*.

## THE BODY, BRAIN, AND MIND

**Impact of Bacteria on Behavior**
Recent explorations of friendly bacteria are the microbiota discussed in Michael Pollan's 2013 article, *Some of My Best Friends Are Germs*:
*http://www.nytimes.com/2013/05/19/magazine/say-hello-to-the-100-trillion-bacteria-that-make-up-your-microbiome.html?ref=magazine&_r=0*

**Parasites that Influence Behavior**
Evidently parasites may influence behavior, emphasizing introversion and extroversion.
*http://www.theatlantic.com/magazine/archive/2012/03/how-your-cat-is-making-you-crazy/8873/*

## Workings of the Brain

Images and explanations of neural firings and workings of the brain:

- http://news.discovery.com/tech/brain-activity-now-in-3d.html
- http://www.youtube.com/watch?v=GIGqp6_PG6k&feature=related
- http://www.youtube.com/watch?v=AdNYIYPHECg
- http://www.youtube.com/watch?v=n9iSzGqKOqM&feature=related
- http://www.youtube.com/watch?v=FZ3401XVYww&feature=related

## SOCIAL MATTERS,

## Dressing Well

A useful book for women available for a few dollars second hand on www.amazon.com is *The Look* by Randolph Duke. There are other related books available there for men when you type in key words such as *dressing well for men* in Books.

## Perils of Paying for Status

A 2012 article in *Scientific American Mind* discusses *The Perils of Paying for Status,*
http://www.scientificamerican.com/article.cfm?id=the-perils-of-paying-for

## PERSONAL AND PROFESSIONAL IMPROVEMENT

### Chinese Word for Crisis
http://en.wikipedia.org/wiki/Chinese_word_for_%22crisis%22

### Demonstration of the Power of Concentration
http://www.flixxy.com/the-incredible-power-of-concentration-miyoko-shida.htm#.UY4ZgYWbKME

### Diaphragmatic Breathing
http://en.wikipedia.org/wiki/Diaphragmatic_breathing

### Imprinting of Ducks
Imprinted ducklings
http://www.youtube.com/watch?v=hwOtEqulb6U&feature=related

### Inspirational Chai
p 32: www.inspirationandchai.com

### Meditation
http://en.wikipedia.org/wiki/Meditation;

### Opportunities to Engage Your Senses
http://www.ted.com/talks/bernie_krause_the_voice_of_the_natural_world.html?utm_source=newsletter_weekly_2013-07-20&utm_campaign=newsletter_weekly&utm_medium=email&utm_content=talk_of_the_week_button

### Plate Tectonics as Metaphor for Behavior
http://www.platetectonics.com/book/page_4.asp

## Power of Habit, Book

http://www.amazon.com/The-Power-Habit-What-business/dp/1400069289/ref=sr_1_1?s=books&ie=UTF8&qid=1332437386&sr=1-1#reader_1400069289

## The Supremes – Stop! In the Name of Love

Supremes' video:
http://www.youtube.com/watch?v=iDPjYZxion8

## Venn Diagrams

Venn diagram: things you enjoy, things you're good at, along with other related images
https://www.google.com/search?q=strengths+images&hl=en&tbm=isch&tbo=u&source=univ&sa=X&ei=t--oUdsK5OTgA9XWgdAN&sqi=2&ved=0CDkQsAQ&biw=1200&bih=568#hl=en&q=venn+diagram+images&tbm=isch

**FOR ADDITIONAL LEARNING, INSIGHT, GUIDANCE, AND ENJOYMENT**
**Available online at** www.amazon.com, often at low second-hand rates.
Many may also be found in libraries.

### Stories of and about living things: people and animals

*A Natural Woman* by Carole King

*Becoming William James* by Howard M. Feinstein

*Emerson: The Mind on Fire* by Robert D. Richardson

*The Once and Future King* by T.H.White

*The Road from Coorain* by Jill Ker Conway

*The Story of Ferdinand* by Munro Leaf

*Theodor SUESS Geisel* by Donald Pease

In addition, explore biographies and autobiographies of your heroes and other people who intrigue you. See Charlie Rose interviews of a wide variety of significant, engaging people at www.charlierose.com

## The value and use of stories

*Lead with a Story: A Guide to Crafting Business Narratives That Captivate, Convince, and Inspire* by Paul Smith

*Narrative Means to Therapeutic Ends* by Michael White and David Epston

*Narrative Truth and Historical Truth: Meaning and Interpretation in Psychoanalysis* by Donald P. Spence

*Public Speaking: Storytelling Techniques for Electrifying Presentations* by Akash Karia

*Stories We Live By: Personal Myths and the Making of the Self* by Dan P. McAdams

*Tell Me a Story* by R.C. Shank

*The Anatomy of Story: 22 Steps to Becoming a Master Storyteller* by John Truby

*The Storytelling Animal: How Stories Make Us Human* by Jonathan Gottschall

*White Gloves: How We Create Ourselves Through Memory* by John Kotre

*Whoever Tells the Best Story Wins: How to Use Your Own Stories to Communicate with Power and Impact* by Annette Simmons

# Selected Bibliography

Often book choices are motivated by immediate, practical needs or a wish for entertainment. These books may offer both. They may inspire your thinking and action, even contribute to your progress. Subject headings are provided to help you focus and make choices, but many books relate to more than one category. *Start by choosing one or two books that interest you.* Feel free to skim or put any choice aside that disappoints in favor of another one that engages.

## Self-Knowledge and Development

Ackerman, Diane. *A Natural History of the Senses.* 1990.

Bayles, David and Ted Orland. *Art and Fear: Observations on the Perils (and Rewards) of Artmaking.* 1993.

Bakewell, Sarah. *How to Live or The Life of Montaigne: In One Question and Twenty Attempts At An Answer.* 2010.

Cottingham, John. *On the Meaning of Life.* 2003.

Crawford, Matthew B. *Shop Class As Soulcraft.* 2009.

Gardner, John W. *Self-Renewal: The Individual and the Innovative Society.* 1995.

Gladwell, Malcolm. *Outliers: The Story of Success.* 2008 or *Talent Is Overrated: What Really Separates World Class Performers from Everybody Else.* by Geoff Colvin. 2010.

Horn, Sam. *POP! Stand Out in Any Crowd.* 2006.

Horney, Karen. *Neurosis and Human Growth: The Struggle toward Self-Realization.* 1950.

Hyatt, Carole and Linda Gottlieb. *When Smart People Fail: Rebuilding Yourself for Success.* 1987.

Kay, John. *Obliquity. Why our goals are best achieved indirectly.* 2011.

Kurs, Katherine, ed. *Searching Your Soul: Writers of Many Faiths Share Their Personal Stories of Spiritual Discovery.* 1999.

May, Rollo. *Man's Search for Himself.* 1973. *The Meaning of Anxiety.* 1977.

Rotundo, E. Anthony. *American Manhood: Transformations in Masculinity from the Revolution to the Modern Era.* 1993.

Seligman, Martin E.P. *Authentic Happiness: Using the New Positive Psychology to Realize Your Potential for Lasting Fulfillment.* 2002.

Shekerjian, Denise. *Uncommon Genius: Tracing the Creative Impulse with 40 Winners of the MacArthur Award.* 1990.

Stone, Elizabeth. *Black Sheep and Kissing Cousins: How Our Family Stories Shape Us.* 1988.

White, T. H. *The Once and Future King.* 1987.

**NOTE:** Also explore biographies, journals, and autobiographies of people whom you find intriguing for inspiration and insight about your own life. Examples: Jill Ker Conway, *The Road from Coorain*; Howard Feinstein, *Becoming William James*; Kathleen Norris, *Dakota: A Spiritual Journey;* Robert Richardson, *Emerson: The Mind on Fire,* Richard Holmes, *Coleridge, I & II* as well as novels that have complex character development.

## Quality of Life and Work

Cohen, Gene D. *The Creative Age: Awakening Human Potential in the Second Half of Life.* 2001.

Csikszentmihalyi, Mihaly. *Finding Flow: The Psychology of Engagement with Everyday Life.* 1997.

Fox, Matthew. *The Reinvention of Work: A New Vision of Livelihood for Our Time.* 1994.

Freedman, Marc. *Encore: Finding Work that Matters in the Second Half of Life.* 2007.

Godin, Seth. *The Dip: A Little Book that Teaches You When to Quit (and When to Stick).* 2007.

Hallowell, Edward. *Crazy Busy.* 2007.

Handy, Charles. *The Age of Paradox.* 1994.

Leider, Richard. *Claiming Your Place at the Fire: Living the Second Half of Your Life on Purpose.* 2004.

Morris, Tom. *True Success: A New Philosophy of Excellence.* 1995.

Nachmanovitch, Stephen. *Free Play: Improvisation in Life and Art.* 1990.

Pink, Daniel. *Free Agent Nation: The Future of Working for Yourself.* 2002.

Robinson, Ken. *The Element: How Finding Your Passion Changes Everything.* 2009.

Schor, Juliet B. *The Overworked American: The Unexpected Decline of Leisure.* 1992.

Schorr, Lisbeth B. *Common Purpose: Strengthening Families and Neighborhoods to Rebuild America.* 1997.

Solomon, Robert C. *Spirituality for the Skeptic: The Thoughtful Love of Life.* 2002.

Vienne, Veronique. *The Art of Doing Nothing: Simple Ways to Make Time for Yourself. The Art of Imperfection.* 1999.

## Thinking and Writing for Personal and Professional Development

Barabasi, Albert-Laszlo. *Linked: How Everything Is Connected to Everything Else and What It Means for Business, Science and Everyday Life.* 2003.

Damasio, Antonio. *Descartes' Error: Emotion, Reason and the Human Brain.* 1994. *The Feeling of What Happens: Body and Emotion in the Making of Consciousness.* 1999.

Fearn, Nicholas. *Zeno and the Tortoise: How to Think Like a Philosopher.* 2001.

Frankl, Viktor E. *The Will to Meaning.* 1969.

Gigerenzer, Gerd. *Gut Feelings: The Intelligence of the Unconscious.* 2007.

Kahneman, Daniel. *Thinking, Fast and Slow.* 2011.

Langer, Ellen J. *Mindfulness.* 1989.

LeDoux, Joseph. *Synaptic Self: How Our Brains Become Who We Are.* 2002.

Jeffrey, Scott. *Creativity Revealed: Discovering the Source of Inspiration.* 2008.

Johnson, Steven. *Where Good Ideas Come From: The Natural History of Innovation.* 2010.

McInerrny, D. Q. *Being Logical: A Guide for Good Thinking.* 2005.

Needleman, Jacob. *Money and the Meaning of Life.* 1994.

Pink, Daniel. *A Whole New Mind: Why Right-Brainers Will Rule the World.* 2006.

Ueland, Brenda. If *You Want to Write: A Book about Art, Independence and Spirit.* 1987.

## Relationships: Professional and Personal

Anderson, Carol et al. *Flying Solo: Single Women in Midlife.* 1995.

Andrews, Frank. *The Art and Practice of Loving.* 1991.

Blyth, Catherine. *The Art of Conversation: A Guided Tour of a Neglected Pleasure.* 2009.

Dimitrius, Jo-Ellan and Mark Mazzarella. *Reading People.* 1999.

Fisher, Helen E. *The Anatomy of Love: The Natural History of Monogamy, Adultery, and Divorce.* 1992.

Ferrazzi, Keith and Tahl Raz. *Never Eat Alone: And Other Secrets to Success, One Relationship at a Time.* 2005.

Fisher, Roger and William Ury. *Getting to Yes: Negotiating Agreement without Giving In.* 1981. Fisher & Brown. *Getting Together.* 1988.

Forni, P. M. *Choosing Civility: The Twenty-five Rules of Considerate Conduct.* 2003.

Goleman, Daniel. *Social Intelligence.* 2006.

Gottman, John. *The Relationship Cure: A 5-Step Guide to Strengthening Your Marriage, Family and Friendships.* 2002.

Gottman, John et al. *Ten Lessons to Transform Your Marriage: America's Love Lab Experts Share Their Strategies for Strengthening Your Relationship.* 2007.

Lewis, Karen. *With or Without a Man: Single Women Taking Control of Their Lives.* 2004.

Marty, Martin E. *The Mystery of the Child (Religion, Marriage, and Family)* 2007.

Sills, Judith. *How to Stop Looking for Someone Perfect and Find Someone to Love.* 2002. *A Fine Romance.* 1987.

Tough, Paul. *How Children Succeed: Grit, Curiosity and the Hidden Power of Character.* 2012.

**YOUR IDEAS FOR BOOKS YOU'VE BEEN PLANNING TO READ:**

_____

_____

_____

_____

**NOTE:** Explore several appealing magazines, journals, and news sources that relate to your interests. Perhaps go beyond them.

# Index

# Endnotes

## Step One: Imagining and Preparing for Your Journey

[1] Janet Rae-Dupree, *If You're Open to Growth, You Tend to Grow*. New York Times, 7.6.08, p. BU3.
[2] Maddi, S. R., & Kobasa, S. C. (1984). *The Hardy Executive: Health under Stress*. Homewood, IL: Dow Jones-Irwin.

## Step Two: Getting Read to Express our Courage

[3] Rob Stein, *Social Networks' Sway May Be Underestimated*, p. A6, Washington Post, May 26, 2008.
[4] Michael E. Zimmerman, *Eclipse of the Self*, p.29-30.
[5] Michael E. Zimmerman, *Eclipse of the Self*, p. xxx.
[6] Rollo May, *Love and Will*, p. 218, 228.
[7] Michael Patrick Hearn, *Ferdinand the Bull's 50th Anniversary*, The Washington Post Book World,    Volume XVI, Number 43, p. 1.
[8] Jonathan Benthall, ed. *The Limits of Human Nature*. p. 97
[9] Hannah Arendt. *The Human Condition*. p. 195.
[10] Hannah Arendt, *The Human Condition*, p. 186.
[11] Majorie Fiske, "Changing Hierarchies of Commitment in Adulthood" in *Themes of Work and Love In    Adulthood*, p. 248-249.
[12] Mahzarim R. Banaji's research reported in The Boston Globe, 2.11.13, *Think you aren't biased? Don't be  so sure.*
[13] David L. Norton, *Personal Destinies: A Philosophy of Ethical Individualism*, p. 195.
[14] David L. Norton, *Personal Destinies: A Philosophy of Ethical Individualism*, p. 194.
[15] Robert C. Solomon, *The Myth and Nature of Human Emotion*, p. xvi., (1976)
[16] Solomon, p. xix.
[17] Solomon, p. xix.
[18] Solomon, p. 132.
[19] Antonio R. Damasio, *Descartes' Error: Emotion, Reason and the Human Brain*, p. 245 (1994)

# Step Three: Identifying Internal Barriers to Progress

[20] William Morris, ed. *The American Heritage Dictionary.* p. 1027
[21] William Morris, ed. *The American Heritage Dictionary.* p. 432
[22] H.H.Gerth and C. Wright Mills, eds., *From Max Weber: Essays in Sociology.* p. 127 (1946)
[23] Urban Digs Interview with Bernard Tschumi, NYTimes Magazine, 6.80.08, p. 42.

# Step Four:  Surpassing Internal Barriers

[24] Frances Bacon, the Major Works, Oxford World Classics, p. 26.
[25] Rollo May, *The Meaning of Anxiety,* p. 198.
[26] Paul Tillich, *The Courage to Be,* p. 42-45.
[27] Melinda Beck, *Anxiety Can Bring Out the Best,* Wall Street Journal, Health and Wellness, June 18, 2012
[28] Ibid, p. 37.
[29] Richard Norman, *The Moral Philosophers: An Introduction to Ethics,* p. 1
[30] Tillich, p. 52.
[31] Senay, Albarracin and Noguchi, *Motivating Goal-Directed Behavior through Introspective Self-Talk: The Role of the Interrogative Form of Simple Future Tense.*  Vol. 21, No 4, pages 499-504; April 2010 *Psychological Science.*  Or Wray Herbert, *Scientific American Mind,* July-August 2010, p. 67.

## Step Five Expressing Your Own Courage

[32] von Clausewitz, *On War,* pages 116, 139, 165.
[33] William Morris, editor, New College Edition, *The American Heritage Dictionary of the English Language,* p. 607.

## Step Six Taking Action

[34] Kegan, Robert. *The Evolving Self. p.* 8.
[35] F. Bradford Wallack. *The Epochal Nature of Process in Whitehead's Metaphysics. p. 69.*
[36] Lavine, T.Z. *From Socrates to Sartre. p. 418.*
[37] Carpenter, Siri. *Body of Thought. p.* 40. Scientific American Mind, January/February, 2011.
[38] Bronowski, J. *The Ascent of Man. p.* 438.
[39] Macquarrie, John. *Existentialism, p. 1-4.*

Made in the USA
Charleston, SC
28 June 2014